The Zombie Apocalypse Guide®

To 3D printing

Designing and printing practical things

Copyright 2013 - 2016, all rights reserved by Clifford T. Smyth

Dedicated to the innovators, makers, and dreamers –

Without which the world would be a very dull place indeed.

Introduction

The purpose of this book is to help you use your 3D printer as a tool for building useful things. My hope is that you will find it an essential volume, enabling you to manufacture things on your desktop that you might otherwise have to purchase, painstakingly craft, or do without.

The Zombie Apocalypse Guide to 3D printing is written with the person who wants to use their printer to make practical, necessary items in mind. Of course this information also applies to items that are purely decorative in nature, but the focus will be on utility oriented issues. The zombie apocalypse paradigm is used as a literary device to set the stage for an emphasis on independence, utility, and practicality.

I will assume in this book that you already have a working knowledge of some kind of 3D design software or are in the process of learning to use it. I will not be giving tips on using specific programs, but rather on principles, paradigms, and processes that apply to all design software and opensource-based fused filament modeling (FFM) printers. To a lesser extent some of these principles may also apply to resin based printers, but the focus will be strongly on FFM designs that use spools of plastic to extrude the printed item layer by layer. To the extent necessary, any specific examples used will feature opensource or free software.

On the impact of 3D Printing

Seldom before in the history of humankind has a technology become so suddenly and widely available, with the potential to fundamentally change the way goods are designed, manufactured, and distributed on a global scale.

The advent of desktop 3D Printing brings with it the potential to empower the average person with unprecedented creative and manufacturing capability, decentralizing a sophisticated means of production with the potential to revolutionize the global supply chain by "shipping" data rather than products. While much of the potential of this technology remains to be realized, the potential social and economic impact of this technology is both far reaching and profound.

The democratization of manufacturing can reduce our environmental footprint and consumption of limited resources, while improving standards of living and creating economically productive opportunities for individuals anywhere on the planet that data can reach.

3d Printing: How does it work?

Although most of you will be familiar with the FFM 3D printing process, this brief introduction will be useful for those that are completely new to the field. Since it is important to understand the printing process in order for this book to be fully utilized, I have provided the following description for those who may need it. If you know how 3D printing works, feel free to skip ahead to chapter 1.

3D printing allows a model in a computer to be made into a physical object automatically. This process starts with the model, either created or downloaded, which is then given to "slicer" software for pre-print processing. In the "slicer", the 3d model is turned into a set of instructions (usually a g-code file) for the printer to follow in order to turn the model into a physical object. This will be done according to supplied specifications about the plastic used to make the model, the desired skin thickness of the finished object, and the solidity of its inner volume, or infill. The generated G-code is then sent to the printer, which creates (prints) the object one layer at a time by extruding plastic from the filament roll onto the print area according to the supplied instructions.

FFM printed structures consist of a stack of layers. The printing process starts with a thin layer of plastic, forming the base of the part, which is extruded onto the print surface or bed. This is done using a small nozzle that extrudes the plastic onto the surface in a line, similar to drawing with a pen.

First, the edges, or perimeters of the base are drawn. This will consist of one or more lines drawn at the outer (and inner, if applicable) "perimeters" or edges of the base layer. Then, to form a solid base, the area inside the perimeter(s) will be "colored in" or infilled with plastic, just like shading an area with a marker or pen. When the base layer is finished, it forms a thin sheet or "slice" of the base of the model a fraction of a millimeter thick.

The next layer or "slice" of the model is then drawn on top of the first, so that the part gradually increases in height, a fraction of a millimeter at a time. In this way, the model is eventually fully developed as a series of sub-millimeter layers, each fused to the one below it.

Although they can be printed solid, 3d printed pieces are often "hollow", with the inner (enclosed) portion filled with a lightweight reinforcing structure, or "infill". This enables 3D printed objects to be much stronger for their weight than with other manufacturing processes, saving time, conserving energy, and using less material.

With infill, the area inside the shell of the model is filled automatically with a geometric pattern, with the density or percentage of the infill being set by the printer operator. The infill adds strength and rigidity to the printed piece, and provides a structure upon which the next layer can be extruded.

The end result is a strong, lightweight piece that can have complex internal structure that would be difficult - or even impossible - to build from a single part using other manufacturing techniques.

Table of Contents

Chapter 1:

Designing and Printing stuff that won't break when you need it to work.. **Page 13**

3D printing opens up a whole new world of possibilities, bringing designs from the virtual into the physical world with unparalleled ease and speed. Representing a true revolution in DIY manufacturing, it is nonetheless burdened by some limitations that are inherent to the technology used.

In this chapter, I will present some of those limitations, and how to work around them to help you to design and build useful, durable things that print quickly and reliably.

Chapter 2:

Prototyping and printing replacement parts, from knobs to triggers.. **Page 44**

One of the handy things that 3D printing is good for is printing replacements for broken or lost parts. In this chapter, I will describe the process of printing replacement parts, and present a case study of a complex part replacement, from templating to final fitting.

Chapter 3:

Making it fit: hinges, latches, joinery, and other useful bits.. **Page 74**

In this chapter, there are examples of different types of hinges, latching mechanisms, and ways of joining printed pieces into larger assemblies. Chapter 3 includes an introduction on fitment clearances, tolerances and printing tips, and features examples of integrating non printed "vitamins" to multiply creative possibilities.

Chapter 4:

Getting the most from your printer .... **Page 97**

A guide to basic adjustment and calibration to get clean, accurate parts from your printer, with pictures and troubleshooting guidelines for common printing problems. Includes Tips on optimizing design and printing parameters for fast, reliable printing. Especially useful for rapid iteration of prototypes, small to medium volume production, and when surface finish is not critical.

Appendix I:

Case studies in practical functional 3D printing .... **Page 129**

Including high speed printing, a demanding two piece assembly with a flexible part, and one piece field replaceable arrow fletchings.

Appendix II:

Printing off the grid – or 3D printing for preppers..... **Page 160**

Living farther away from supply chains opens up new levels of practicality for 3D printing, as well as some new challenges. Here we address the critical issue of printing from intermittent, improvised, or alternative power systems.

Glossary: ....Page 173

A list of terms in a specialized field of usage or discipline, with accompanying definitions. Often found in the back of a book, explaining unusual words or expressions found in the text. In this case, pertaining to terms and concepts peculiar to 3D printing, with summarized discussion of the topic in some cases.

Intentionally blank

Chapter 1:

Designing and Printing stuff that won't break when you need it to work

Nothing can ruin your zombie ambush as quickly as when a critical tool fails to perform as required. As Murphy's Law dictates, this seems to occur mostly at the worst possible times, so it's important that the designs we print are robust and up to the task at hand.

Basics: form and material

This is pretty obvious, but nonetheless bears mentioning. Knowing that the finished part will be made of plastic (unless you wish to cast it in metal, using a lost - PLA process or something), consider whether the design will be durable enough to perform the intended task. Is your design idea based on a wooden or plastic item you have seen? If so, it will probably work, perhaps with slight modification. Was the original made of titanium or hardened steel? If so, the design may require major adaptation, and parts of it may have to be of a harder material than you can print.

Think about the stresses the object may be subjected to in the operational environment. Many times, difficult applications may require you to draft, print, test, and redesign your model, iterating on the design until a workable version is created. In the case studies given in *Appendix I* (page 128) you will find examples of this process.

You should consider the material used to print your model with the purpose of the part in mind. ABS is very durable and somewhat flexible, at around 4000 PSI printed tensile strength under ideal circumstances. PLA is stronger, at around 6000 PSI, but is less flexible and shatters more easily. Nylon filaments give excellent flexibility and 4000 - 8000 PSI of tensile strength, but are problematic to print due to high shrinkage. Some nylons, such as Taulman's® 910 (taulman3D.com), are specially formulated for 3D printing and offer an excellent combination of strength and flexibility for demanding applications. PET and PETG filaments offer sort of a half-way point between PLA and Nylon on the spectrum, with strength approaching Nylon but less flexibility. TPU and similar filaments give extreme flexibility - similar to rubber – but are picky about extruder drive systems.

In addition to the basic categories, special filaments abound - including wood, metal, and carbon fiber reinforced varieties. Electrically conductive, glow in the dark, and color changing filaments are also available. It is important to choose the correct material for the task at hand, but in practice material choice sometimes just comes down to what you have, so keeping the material you will be printing with in mind can be a critical part of a successful design.

Note that the approximate printed strengths given here are in the X-Y plane of the print bed. Vertical or Z-axis strengths will be lower in tension...more on this later.

Print orientation and strength

Parts made using the FFM (FDM) process are stronger in some directions than in others. This is due to imperfect adhesion between printed layers. This directional or *anisotropic* structural strength superficially resembles the properties of wood. With wood, there is one strong axis, along the grain of the growth of the tree from which it was cut. In the other two axes, most wooden objects are comparatively weak. With FFM parts, there are two axes of strength and only one axis of comparative weakness – the Z- (vertical) axis.

Despite the differences in the characteristics of wooden and FFM printed objects, the grain characteristics of wood can act as a useful analogy in guiding design choices.

As mentioned earlier, the Z (or perpendicular to the print bed) axis is relatively weak in tensile strength due to sub-optimal interlayer adhesion. This effect is rather dramatic, and the X-Y tensile strength of a part is often 4-10 times as high as the Z-axis strength, all other factors being equal.

It is almost always worthwhile to redesign structural parts so that they can be printed flat on the print bed, even if it means breaking them down into multiple sections. *This is possibly the most important factor to keep in mind while designing for 3D printing.* There is more about this coming up in a few paragraphs, in the section on *Printability*.

Printing Parameters: strength, speed, and finish

Aside from material and orientation, the other significant factor that will affect your printed parts' strength is the printing parameters. For printing parameters to predictably control print characteristics, it is important to be sure that your printer is properly calibrated (*see calibration, Page 106*) and that you have measured your supply filament diameter accurately. Aside from these basics, you will want to have a level print bed and a proper Z-height adjustment.

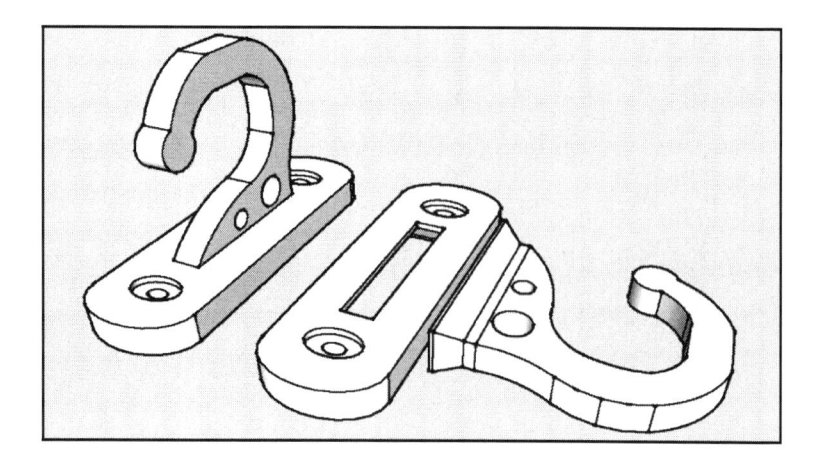

Two designs for a wall hook. The one on the left will print in one piece, but will require support, more time to print, and use more material. The two piece version on the right can be quickly and reliably printed and assembled, and will support much more weight than the one piece version. (Functional design for 3d printing)

The most important printing parameters are typically layer height, number of perimeters (the wall thickness on the x-y "sides" of the print), top and bottom surface thickness, infill type, and infill density.

For structurally non-critical prints, a layer height of half of your nozzle diameter, a perimeter thickness of two perimeters (or 2 times your nozzle diameter) and a top/bottom thickness of two times your layer height usually works out well. In many cases, shorter layer heights can improve print finish, especially with curved upper or overhanging surfaces. Shorter layer heights reduce aliasing errors (stepping) on sloped upper and lower surfaces, but can markedly increase printing time.

The other major parameter is infill. Infill below 25% can give an unpredictable top finish, so 25% is a good starting point. For non structural parts 30% gives good durability without wasting plastic, and this can be gainfully increased for more strength up to around 60%.

After 60 percent or so, you can usually gain more strength for the plastic and print time used by increasing the perimeter width, the top and bottom thickness, or redesigning the part altogether to use less than 60% infill while providing the required strength. If the part must be as strong as possible but cannot be redesigned, it is usually better to go with 95%-98% infill than 100%, as small calibration errors or filament variation can cause the print to "overfill" leading to a nozzle crash and ruining the print.

Overhangs and bridges: the supporting factors

One of the fundamental limitations of the layer-by layer 3D manufacturing process used by FFM 3D printers is that overhangs are problematic to print. This is because overhanging structures have no supporting structure below to support the material being extruded. Unsupported, they tend to fall downward causing sagging, drooping, or even complete failure of the print.

In cases where overhanging structures are not adequately supported by previous layers or the print bed, support material may be automatically generated by the slicer, depending on your settings.

Support is needed when printing structures where a printing layer will not be adequately supported by the layer below it. In this example, an arch (inset) requires support material to support the center section while printing. Turning the arch on its end would eliminate the need for support material, making printing faster and more reliable. (Illustration by author)

In some cases with unsupported structures, there is another structure nearby that can be attached to, like a bridge between two blocks. If the structure is nearby (usually less than 3cm depending on your printer and cooling setup) plastic can be successfully extruded across the gap without support.

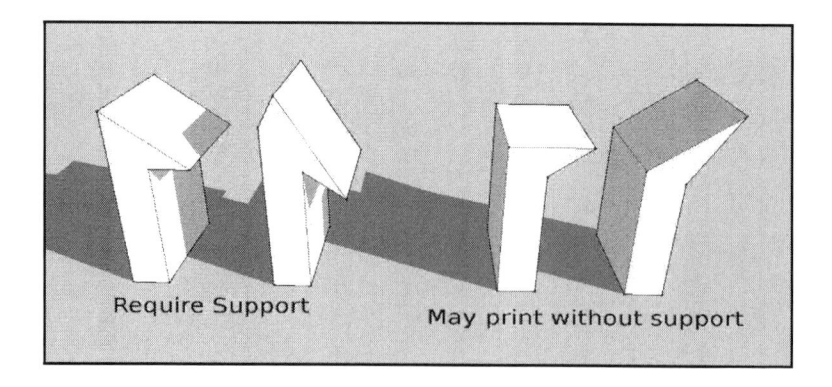

In this drawing, four examples of overhanging structures are shown. The two examples on the left cannot be printed successfully without support material. This is because their overhanging part extends horizontally or downward, so that the printed material of the overhang would be extruded over free space, drooping toward the print bed. In the examples on the right, printing will probably be successful, because each layer will be at least partly supported by the layer below it. (Functional design for 3d printing)

This is called bridging. Bridging is usually not problematic for distances under a centimeter, but reliability drops as the distance increases. The maximum distance you can bridge will depend on many factors including the type of plastic used, cooling, and print speeds. Normally it is best to avoid bridging large distances when practical, but bridges of less than a centimeter are pretty reliable.

Aside from the distance limitation, the other critical factors in bridging are that the sides of the bridge must be straight, and the bridge must cross the entire span in one printing layer. In practice, this generally means that the bottom (first) layer of the bridge must be horizontal, with little or no inclination. After the span is accomplished, the upper surface can have any form desired as it will be supported by the layers below it. The bridge also cannot bend or turn in mid span, as there is no way to support the change in direction. This is why the sides of the bridge must be straight.

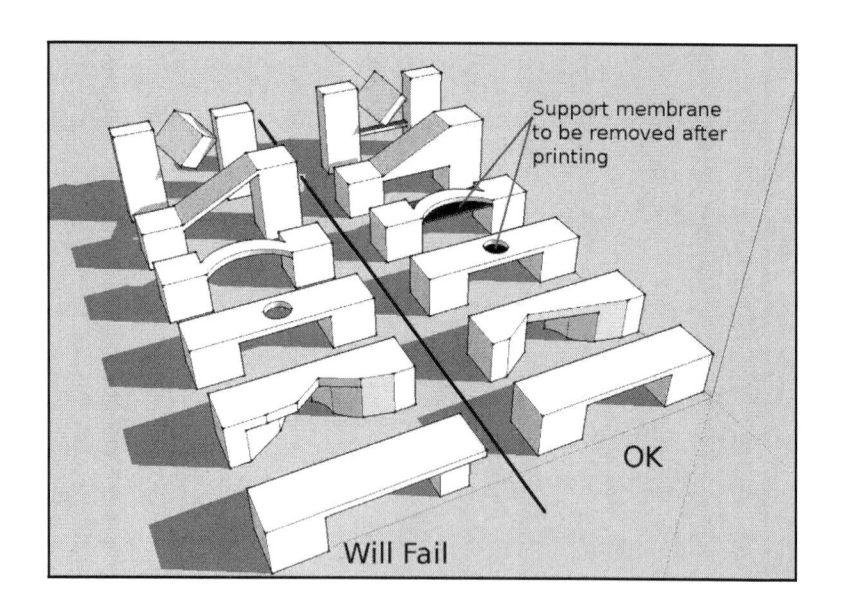

Comparison of structures that should successfully bridge without additional support (right) with ones that will not (left). Note the non-straight, unsupported or incomplete bridge areas on the left. (Functional design for 3d printing)

Optimizing for printability

Once you have worked out the basic design and size requirements, the next thing to consider is printability. Objects that print quickly and reliably are said to be more "printable" than ones that take longer and / or are more likely to fail.

All other things being equal, a model that prints quickly will also print more reliably than a slower printing version of the same model. This is because a print that has less wasted motion and excess complexity will print faster and presents less opportunity for failure.

For reliable printing, minimize complexity and lay everything flat on the bed if possible. Bridging and fragile support structures are common culprits in print failure. Tall vertical structures are weaker, generally less reliable to print, and easily dislodge from the print bed.

For speed, the primary design considerations are horizontal orientation, layer height, and minimum overall structure and complexity. Gently rounded corners require less acceleration braking, and eliminating support requirements just gives you that much less to print. Beyond that, minimizing complexity generally improves printing times and outcomes.

Part orientation should be optimized to reduce or eliminate the need for bridging or support whenever possible. One example of refactoring a design to reduce support requirements and improve printability is a doll house table: if printed upright, it will require support and be very prone to failure. If printed upside-down, no support would be required, but the fragile legs would be unreliable and slow to print.

If the tabletop is printed upside-down, with sockets for the legs, and the legs are printed separately laying flat on the print bed, the table will print quickly, reliably, and with no waste. Not only that, the legs will be much stronger and print finish quality will be much better.

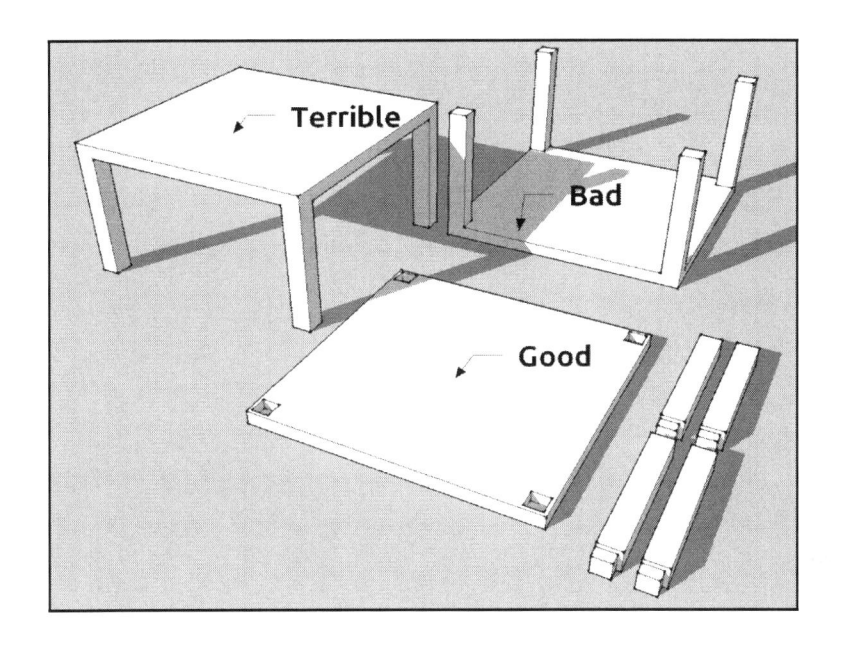

3 different versions of the same model, demonstrating design reorientation and refactoring to optimize printability (Illustration by author)

If your model cannot be reoriented or refactored (subdivided) to print without support, it can sometimes be useful to design in your own support structures. This is especially the case for an item that you will be printing in large quantities, because it can result in significant time and material savings over automatically generated support while simplifying the printing process.

Another case for designing your own support structures is where automatically generated support may be difficult or impossible to remove without damaging your model.

When designing your own support, a small gap must be left between the support structure and the rest of the model to facilitate removal. 0.3mm to 0.5mm is usually sufficient for this, although for very small nozzle sizes a smaller gap may be appropriate.

An advanced solution for support that avoids most removal problems is to use dual extrusion and dissolvable support materials, but that is beyond the scope of this book. This and other more advanced design topics are covered more thoroughly in my other (designer oriented) book, *Functional design for 3d printing*, available online or at your local bookseller through Ingram or Baker & Taylor publishers.

An example of designed-in support (dark grey). Note the small separation between the support and the supported tab. This support structure will print and support more consistently than most automatically generated support. With a gentle press, the support snaps out cleanly and easily in one piece. Designing in support instead of using automatically generated structures is usually not necessary for one-off prints, but can be very practical for things that will be printed many times like this extruder assembly. (Illustration by author)

29

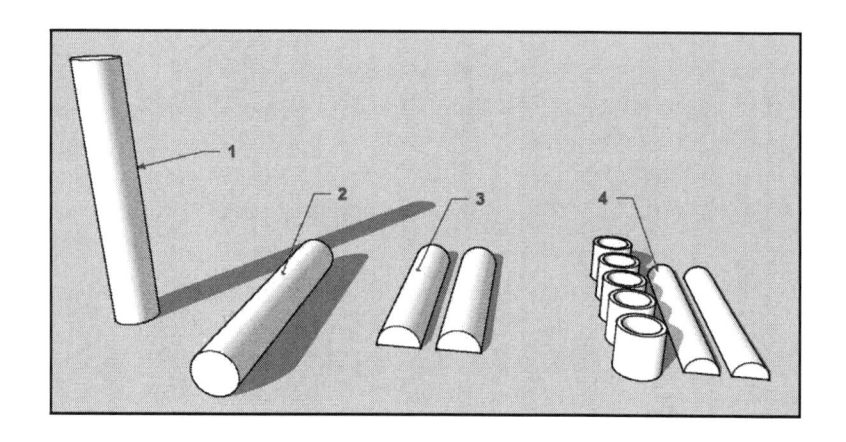

Print orientation and refactoring preparation for similar models. (Illustration by author)

Print orientation and design refactoring

In the following exercise, consider 4 approaches to a long solid cylinder, from left to right. In these examples, the nozzle width is 0.4mm, with a 0.2mm layer height and a 60mm/sec print head speed.

All of these models are roughly equivalent, but each will print with different characteristics.

Model 1:

> If cosmetic finish is important and strength requirements are minimal, the simple upright cylinder might be a good option if the cylinder is not excessively narrow. There could be reliability problems with the print because of the tall narrow profile, but with good bed adhesion or if printed using adhesion aids (such as a skirt) specified in the slicer, it should generally work.
>
> Example time would be 38 minutes, with 2.53g of filament used.

Model 2:

> If cosmetic finish is not important, the horizontally oriented cylinder could work, and should give reasonable strength and low printing times. Its principal disadvantage is that it may have to be printed using support, and the overhanging underside of the rising surfaces is likely to have a poor finish.

Finished part strength should be fairly good, and although roundness might be an issue, it would work in many situations.

Example time would be 12 minutes, with 3.13g of filament used. If support were required, time would jump a half minute or so, with 3.2g of material consumed.

Model 3:

A generally superior solution to example 2, printing in two halves improves the roundness and finish while eliminating the need for support – improving print reliability and speed. It should be slightly stronger than example 2 as well, but will require adhesive to glue the two halves together. In many cases, this is a good compromise and offers the fastest, most reliable print.

In our example, the print time is just under 12 minutes, with 2.99g of plastic used.

Model 4:

> This is the strongest version of the cylinder, with a horizontal core girdled by circumferential rings. This will be quite a bit stronger than any of the others, and will have a nice round external profile as well.
>
> At 20 minutes, it isn't the fastest, but it's still about half the time of the other circumferential shell option. Post printing assembly is somewhat complex, but if properly dimensioned the assembly can be pressed together without glue. In this case, a 0.2mm gap was left between the core diameter and the rings, which should give an interference fit in most cases, but for optimal strength glue (or solvent welding), would be used as well.
>
> 3.58g of plastic is used in this example.

As you can see, time to print, strength, and printing reliability can vary drastically depending on the structure and orientation of the model.

The most striking difference that can be seen in this exercise is the effect of part orientation on speed. Tall, narrow objects have short extrusion runs, and lots of time consuming repositioning moves. Movements translate into errors, so reliability is also compromised. Even if the cylinder was broken into 5 short cylinders, time would still be over 25 minutes, and getting them aligned and glued would be extra effort as well. Emphasizing horizontal structures in your design pays off in many ways, but speed and strength are the big wins.

Slicer (mis)behavior

An often overlooked factor in the design-for-printing process is the post design / pre-print processing of the model. After successfully designing a solid to be printed (the model must be closed as a solid to ensure proper printing), it needs to be processed, or sliced, into a series of layer by layer instructions for the printer to follow. The settings used for this process -

slicing - can have a significant effect on printing complexity, even when processing the same model.

In the following image, we see the result of two different settings in CURA for the same model. With 0.5mm wall thickness, tool path complexity is increased in comparison to a 1mm wall thickness setting. Both settings will produce nearly identical prints in this case, but the 0.5mm wall thickness will print slower, with a higher probability of failure.

When using a slicer that allows you to preview the tool path as was done in these pictures, it is often useful to browse through the layers looking for any unnecessary complexity or gross slicer errors. Sometimes, the problem is actually an error in the model, but be on the lookout for poor compatibility between your model and your slicer settings.

Often you may be designing something that will be printed by someone else. In these cases, it can be useful to provide instructions regarding the ideal settings for printing your design.

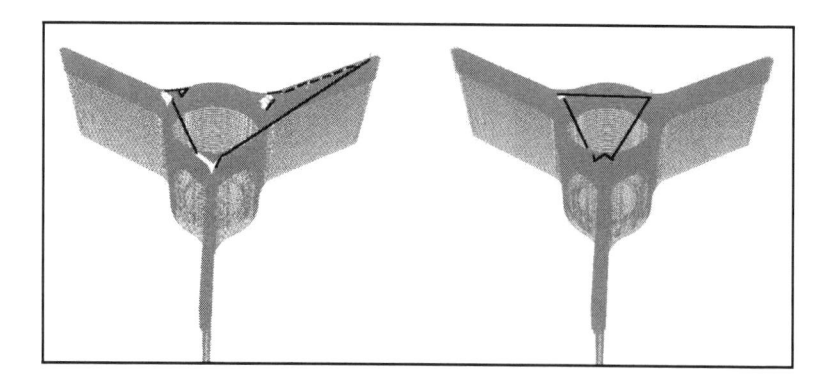

Identical models, sliced in CURA using different wall thickness settings. The black lines represent non-printing repositioning moves. In both cases, the fins will be solid with no empty space, but in the example on the right, there is less wasted tool movement, so the print will complete more quickly with a better finish, and with a reduced chance of print failure. (Illustration by author)

A special case for layer height and print finish...*this is going to get a little technical:*

If your printer uses a threaded rod Z-axis drive as most printers do, it is best to ensure that the layer height used when slicing your model for printing is an *exact* multiple of your per-(micro)step Z motion. This will help you to avoid banding and layer artifacts.

For example, if you are using a 5mm threaded rod Z axis screw, the thread pitch on that rod is probably 0.8mm, so each full turn of the rod will give a 0.8mm change in Z. If you are using a common 1.8° stepper motor, each step rotates the motor 1.8 degrees, so there are 200 steps in a full revolution. (360 / 1.8 = 200)

It follows then that each step will be 1/200th of the thread pitch, or 0.004mm Z height change per step. (0.005*0.8=0.004). Your best results will be achieved using layer heights that are multiples of 0.004mm, so 0.2mm , or 0.1mm will give good results, but 0.25mm will likely result in some banding artifacts, as 0.25 / .004 = 62.5 so every other layer will contain an extra motor step of height, causing some banding.

Sometimes, slicer errors can cause significant defects, as seen in this print. Here, the slicer left a gap in the wall where the thickness should have been 0.5mm, the nozzle width on the printer. In this case, a redesign of the model was required to allow it to slice correctly. The periodic banding (ripple) in the upper half is caused by a mismatch between the layer height setting and the Z axis threaded rod pitch, while the extreme ripple near the bottom is a result of slicer errors. Taking a quick look at the tool path would have saved me the trouble of printing this failed piece. (Photo by author)

If you are using microstepping on your Z-axis motors, the same calculations apply, but you should use steps multiplied by microsteps-per-step instead of plain steps in the equations.

Determining failure and working loads

Warning: Making life safety critical items with your 3D printer may result in an unscheduled departure from the realm of the living

If the item is critical, its failure load should be determined as part of the prototyping process. The failure load is the load at which the item breaks completely, begins to deform so that failure is imminent, or deforms so that it can no longer perform its intended function. To determine the working load limit, a test to failure of at least 5 samples should be performed.

The test should closely approximate the use environment. If there will be motion, the *worst case* motion should be incorporated into the test as accurately as possible.

The test should utilize the same printer, printing file, and print material for each test model as will be used in the production model. If the test will be formalized into a load rating, the failure loads of each test should be recorded and the mean and standard deviation noted. The calculated minimum failure strength (MFS) of the printed item can be considered to be approximately the mean failure load minus 3 times the standard deviation of the tested failure loads. This will provide a confidence level of 95% for the MFS rating. If a higher confidence level is required, more test samples must be used.

A way of estimating a nominal working load limit is to divide the calculated minimum failure strength (MFS) by a safety factor of 3 for static, non-moving items, and by 4 to 10 for moving or lifting items. For especially violent motion, safety factors may need to be even higher.

If the item will be subjected to long term heavy loading, testing should ideally be done out to twice the expected load times to test for progressive failure. Any significant -progressive- deformation should be interpreted as part failure.

If the item involves life-safety, wider margins and more rigorous testing is indicated, of course.

CRITICAL NOTE: These working load estimates will only be valid when using precisely the same printer, the same batch of material, the same calibrations, and precisely the same printing file (g-code). Any changes in these parameters and all bets are off. At this point you might be getting the idea that printing heavily loaded objects for life safety critical applications is a bad idea.....and this is definitely the case. If you have other options, examine them closely before betting a life on improvised engineering.

(Caption for photo on next page)

42

(Caption for photo on previous page)

An example of improvised testing. A tarp clip is subjected to increasing loads up until the point of failure. In this case, the bucket was filled with water and when that failed to produce deformation or breakage, scrap metal and rock was used as a weight instead.

Ultimately, the clip shown failed at 32.6kg. Over several tests, it was determined that the clips failed around 33.4kg, with the standard deviation being 2.1kg. That gives us a calculated minimum failure strength of 33.4 – (2.1x3) = 27.1kg. From this, a working load limit of 6.7kg was calculated, using a safety factor of 4.

The otherwise identical clip printed in the Z direction rather than flat on the bed supported less than half of the load of the X-Y printed part before failing. (Functional design for 3d printing)

Chapter 2

Fixing stuff: Prototyping and printing replacement parts

A frequent and practical use of 3D printing is replacing broken or missing parts in everyday objects. Whether your machete needs a new handle or your salvaged chainsaw is missing a critical detail, a 3D printed part can get you back on task when the chips are down.

First, some basic modeling paradigms

Most 3D printing projects start with a 3D model. While it is certainly possible to painstakingly write the direct instructions (g-code) for the printer and have it execute them, this is not the normal 3D printing workflow. Usually, the workflow is: *Concept> Design> Slicing (preprint processing)> Printing.*

Slicing is where the model is processed by the preprint (slicing) software to generate a list of commands for the printer to execute which results in the printing of a facsimile of the design. Many opensource and closed source slicers are available, but the examples in this book use the popular free, easy to use CURA software.

No matter what you plan on designing, you are probably going to end up using some type of 3D CAD or modeling program. For most applications the simplest way to develop functional designs is using an interactive 3D workspace tool, and most popular 3D CAD programs fall into this category.

The two main design paradigms used in interactive 3D design are prism extrusion and wireframe lofting. Most 3D CAD programs allow both, and most models are developed using a combination of these (and other) methods.

It is worth noting that no matter what method is used to develop your design, it should be represented as a closed or 'watertight' solid.

Two conceptually similar interpretations of a simple coffee cup. The one on the left cannot be printed, because it is not a solid, and has no interior volume in which to extrude plastic to make it a physical object. (Illustration by author)

For example, if modeling a cup, it needs to have separate inner and outer surfaces that join at the rim and the base. It should have a closed interior volume. If it does not, then there is no place to put plastic, as the walls themselves have a zero volume. Some slicing software will attempt to compensate for errors of this category, but the results are not reliably consistent with the intention of the design.

Seeing the world through a Prism:

The prism extrusion paradigm of modeling sees the world as an assembly of 2 dimensional (flat) structures stretched (extruded) up into a third dimension to form the basic building blocks of the design universe.

The process of modeling using this method goes roughly as follows:

1. *Sketch the main 2D outline of your model using basic 2D drawing tools (lines, curves, polygons).*
2. *Extrude the drawn shape to give it the desired profile.*
3. *Sketch more 2D shapes on the surfaces of the part you just extruded*
4. *go back to step 2 until finished*

With this method, the desired model is developed out of a series of prismatic components "grown" or "cut" from the original outline, on its various vertices and sub-vertices.

This technique is a very rapid way to develop relatively complex forms quickly and accurately. It works very well for prototyping from a set of dimensions, and many manufactured parts fall into this design category in their physical manifestation. The principle disadvantage of this method is that it is difficult to create freeform or sculpted "organic" 3 dimensional objects, as the prismatic model tends to involve a series of planar surfaces and angular forms.

Another variation of this technique is using 3D "primitives" or basic shapes (such as cubes, cylinders, cones, and spheres) and adding them together to create the desired form. The parts or combinations can be extruded (stretched) and deformed as needed. Other primitives or assemblies can be merged into parts being designed, then "subtracted" to cut out undesired sections.

The progressive development of a knob using prismatic modeling. Note how in each step, material is added or removed by prismatic sections. To make new sections, a figure is drawn on a face of the previous step, and then used to create a new structure or cut some of the previous away. This is accomplished by simply selecting and pushing/pulling the surface of each section with the pointer to make it extend or retract. (Illustration by author)

Wireframe Lofting

The term "lofting" came from the time of sailing ships, where a design would be laid out full size or to scale in an open building space (often a loft) so that measurements could be taken and drawings and tables of dimensions made to facilitate the building of the ship. Sails were also dimensioned and cut in a similar way. When we "loft" a wireframe structure, we follow a similar procedure, sketching out a rough form and progressively adjusting and filling in the details until the desired result is achieved.

Lofting a wireframe design starts with a two dimensional profile sketch, much as with prismatic modeling. In this case since the desired form is not an evolution of a prism, it must be manually defined.

A common method is to sketch the main profile first, then the rough profiles in the two perpendicular planes. After that, profiles can be added at different 'sections', reflecting the overall form of the desired object. Usually this is done along the longest axis. After the form is developed, the profiles are stitched together at their vertices, forming a wire frame model. From the wire frame, a skin is then defined, either manually be inserting vertices and forming planes, or using automatic "wrapping" algorithms, depending on the software used. Once the model is properly defined as a solid, it can then be processed for printing.

In this simple example of wireframe modeling, you can see the development of a model aircraft canopy from a basic outline to final form. In each step, profiles are added and finally connected to form a solid. In the final step, some of the vertices are repositioned with the pointer to achieve the desired final form. (Illustration by author)

There are many excellent tutorials available online for most CAD programs, and I encourage the beginner to use these and to take the time to familiarize themselves with whatever modeling software they will be using.

A word on parametric modeling:

Parametric modelers (like openSCAD) are powerful tools for developing mathematically or algorithmically defined shapes. A common use case for parametric modeling is screws, nuts, fan blades, or other similar repeating forms. These types of objects are where parametric modelers really outshine interactive modeling software. Some interactive modelers incorporate parametric capabilities, giving the designer the best of both worlds.

 Although any shape can be defined using parametric or scripted modelers, their biggest advantage lies in their parametric capabilities. This allows the designer to create, for example, a threaded nut using only its dimensions and characteristics, described in a script. No "drawing" need be done to describe the part. After the nut is described, it can then be modeled with different thread pitches, sizes, outer profiles (hex vs. star, for example) and thread types by just tweaking the parameters that control these features rather than redesigning it from scratch. In its more advanced manifestations, parametric modeling allows the designer to specify any parameter in the design as a variable item, allowing the instant generation of multiple design variations.

For example, a toy car could be modeled using a parametric modeler. The same model could generate a toy car with varying wheel heights and sizes, varying numbers of doors (stretch limo feature), varying numbers of axles, various fastener sizes for putting it together (metric or imperial), and a host of other customizable features. All of these features could be changed without having to redesign the model, and could even be reconfigured by a complete novice, loading the software into a design customizer which would display simple slider or checkbox controls to facilitate the feature adjustments.

It is important to note that the designer does not have to anticipate all of the variations, but merely to incorporate the possibility of the variations into the design.

I have provided this introduction to parametric modeling to encourage the ambitious reader to investigate this advanced and powerful tool further, but as an advanced and specialized technical subject it is beyond the scope of this book. For this reason, I won't be using parametric modeling in my examples but will rather focus on the more accessible and intuitive interactive design paradigm.

Prototyping for repair:

In many cases, an original part may be available to take measurements from. If this is the case, first determine which measurements are critical, and which can (or should be) changed without causing problems with fitting or using the part. Take careful measurement of any critical dimensions, especially cutouts for shafts, fasteners, or other structures. For this process, a set of calipers is nearly indispensable. A ruler will do in a pinch, but accurate measurements are the key to accurate fitting, so a small investment on-line for even a cheap set will be money well spent.

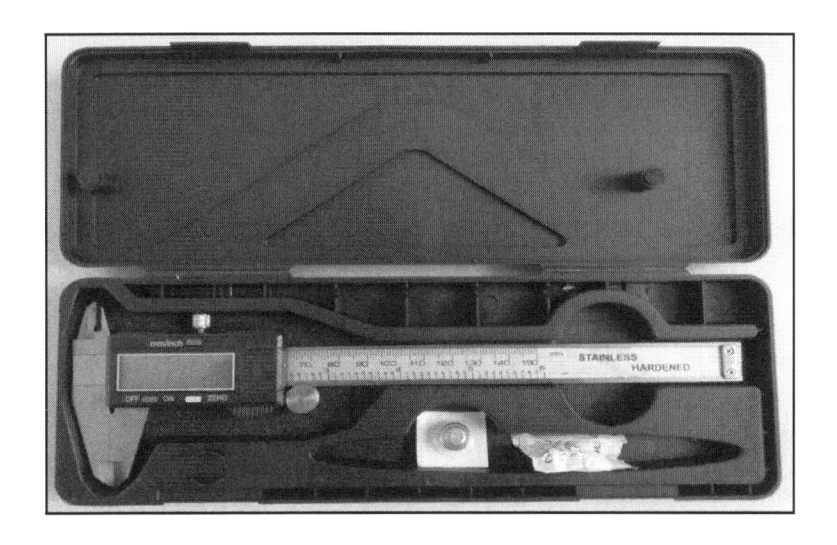

A set of digital or dial calipers can really come in handy, simplifying measurements for creating replacement parts and making calibration of printed objects much more accurate. (Photo by author)

If the shape of the part is complex and the original part is not available, it is often desirable to use a piece of cardboard or plastic to cut out a 2-d mock-up of the part - or even several at different elevations. This will make your prototypes more likely to fit, and less work will have to be done adjusting and reprinting the design.

After the mock up fits correctly (if used), draft the design using your 3D modeling software using the dimensions of the old part or your mock up.

Critical dimensions should be given a 0.2mm allowance for overextrusion, as a starting point. For example, to make a cube exactly 20mm across, it should be drawn at 19.6mm, giving 0.2mm allowance on each side to accommodate overextrusion. If an 8mm shaft will fit loosely onto the part, the design should incorporate an 8.4mm (0.2mm per side) hole. For tight fitting parts, 0.1mm may be sufficient.

Depending on your print settings and the decisions your slicer makes when writing out the build instructions, these dimensions may require some adjustment for different situations. Usually 0.2mm to 0.3mm gives good results, but especially with taller layer heights or nozzle overloading (more on this in chapter 3 and chapter 5) this figure may have to be increased. If a part will be threaded using a tap (or a hot bolt) the exact dimension without additional allowance may be adequate, or less allowance may be required.

When fitting two printed parts together, remember that each one should have an overextrusion allowance, so with a 0.2mm allowance, a 10mm nominal printed peg will need 10.8mm hole to fit. Two side by side parts *each* need a 0.2mm fitment allowance. A tight friction fit can be obtained by removing some or all of the allowance from one of the parts.

A shaft coupler. The design must flex a little when tightening, without deforming. By making the sections thin where they need to flex, stresses on the plastic are reduced making the part "springy" so that it is not permanently deformed from bending. A part like this is evolved from a 2-d template (foreground), and then details such as the screw holes and recesses incorporated into the basic design after it is "extruded" upward in the modeling software. (Illustration by author)

Here, a knob incorporates a flexible "tongue" to keep it snug on its shaft. Notice the guard around the tongue to prevent overextension, protecting it from being bent to the point of permanent deformation or breakage. To quickly draw something like this, a 2D outline of the knob grip is extruded upward, and then the shaft gripping detail is then drawn on top and likewise extruded, forming the two step design seen here. (Illustration by author)

Chainsaw Repair for undead preparedness

Where I demonstrate the design and printing of a critical part to repair an electric chainsaw.

When I first saw it, the chainsaw had been taken to pieces and left for dead some time ago by a friend of mine. I saw it on his boat, and asked him about it. He told me it was now missing a piece and asked me if I wanted it. He said he had tried to find a replacement part, but since the saw was no longer being made or supported by the manufacturer there were none available unless I could find one used. Gazing lovingly at the greasy sack of parts, I of course took the bag into my gentle care and brought it home with me.

Once home, I looked it over and it seemed complete except for the trigger switch....an easy fix for someone with a 3D printer, I considered, warming to the task. With visions of a mounting an electric chainsaw zombie defense with my soon to be repaired battle saw, I began to sort out how to go about getting started.

As often occurs, I was faced with the task of designing a replacement part with no original part to start from. In the case where a broken original is available the process can be easier, but in many cases the form of the missing part can be imagined from the function and location it serves.

I find that the most important tools for a project like this (besides drafting software and a 3D printer) are a precision measuring device such as a set of calipers, a bit of cardboard, and a good pair of scissors. This will make it trivially easy to make template prototypes to check clearances, shapes, and sizes.

First, I installed the switch and wires into the handle so that I could imagine what form a new trigger would have to have to activate the switch.

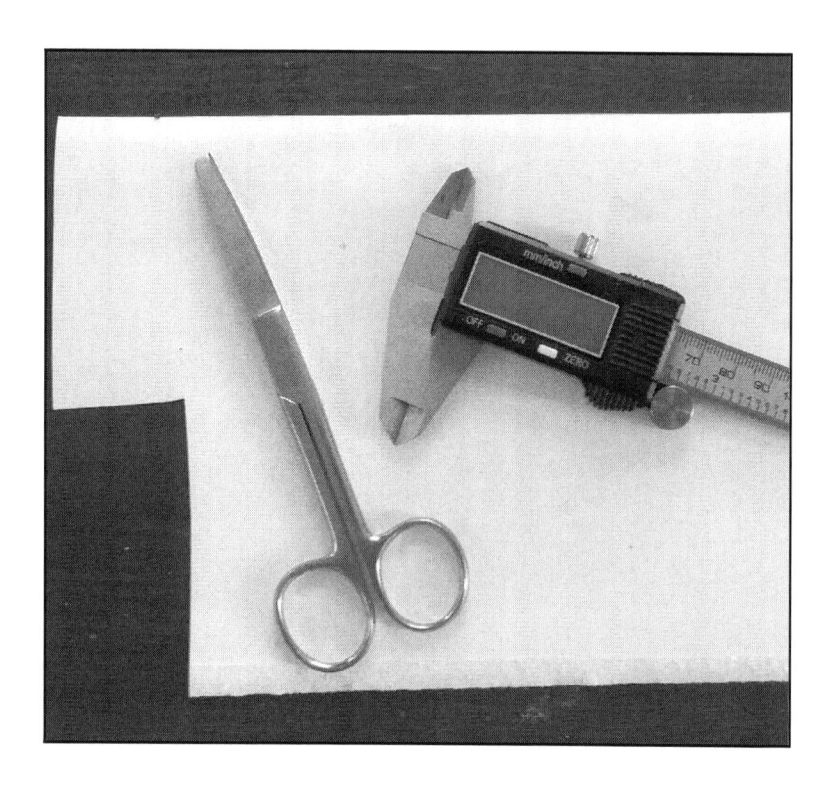

Aside from your 3D printing setup, a few simple tools will make fitting a prototype template quick and easy. (Photo by author)

I started fiddling around with paper card cutouts until I got something of about the right shape. After fitting and refining the paper mock-up, I checked it through its full range of motion to be sure it would depress and release the little micro switch. I then verified that it would remain captive in the handle in the correct position when released, even if it was being knocked around a bit.

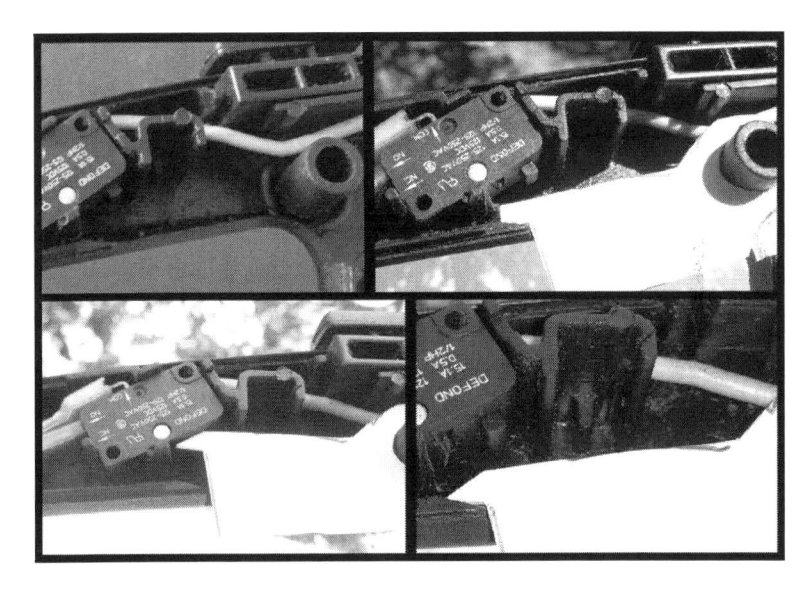

The process of creating a template for the prototype: Preparation, initial fitting, revision, and final checking for fit and functional shape. In cases like this, it is often practical to think in terms of expanded 2-dimensional shapes or prisms. (Photo by author)

At this point I noted that the micro switch had a fairly weak spring. I felt that it was not strong enough to prevent accidental operation of the saw, and certainly not strong enough to return the trigger to the off position reliably if the operator was wearing gloves.

A quick look around my workshop revealed that I had no suitable small springs lying around, so I started thinking about how to integrate a plastic spring into the design. I decided to use ABS for the print material, as I have much more experience with plastic springs in ABS than in other materials.

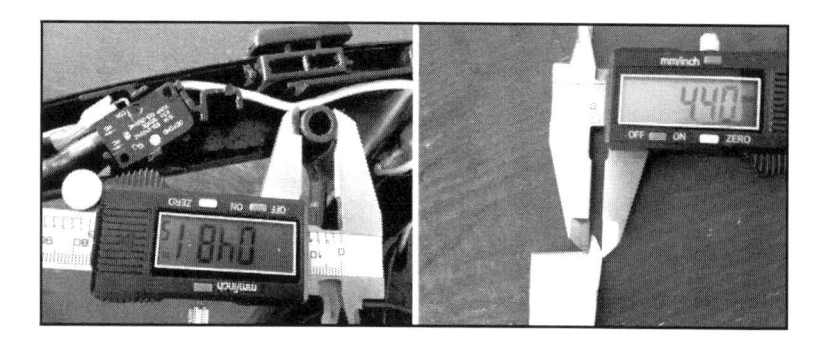

Taking precise measurements from both the template and the part environment is the key to getting good results. (Photo by author)

After taking some critical measurements from the saw handle and the paper mock up, I began drawing out the part in Trimble Sketchup - one of my favorite programs for simple jobs like this despite its many, many shortcomings as an engineering cad program. (Don't judge me). I printed a short version, interrupting the print after about 10 layers to test the fit and position of the spring I designed. It fit well and looked like it should work, so I printed another full part.

As print speed (I'm impatient) and strength were the only critical parameters, I printed at 0.5mm nozzle width and 0.3mm layer height. I have a 0.4mm nozzle on this machine, so 0.5 is slightly over my actual nozzle width. In general up to 20% over your actual nozzle width will give good results, and better overlap between extrusion lines. By "nozzle overloading" you can gain part strength and printing speed at the expense of a surface finish and dimensional accuracy.

It's important to note that you need to draw your part slightly smaller than the desired dimensions of the finished piece due to overextrusion.

Stopping mid print after ten layers, a partial print waits to be tested for proper fit before printing the final piece. (Photo by author)

Normally, about 0.2mm on each side (not top and bottom) is about right, but when you use a setting larger than your actual nozzle size like I did in this case, this can go up to 0.3 or even 0.5mm for accurate finished part dimensions.

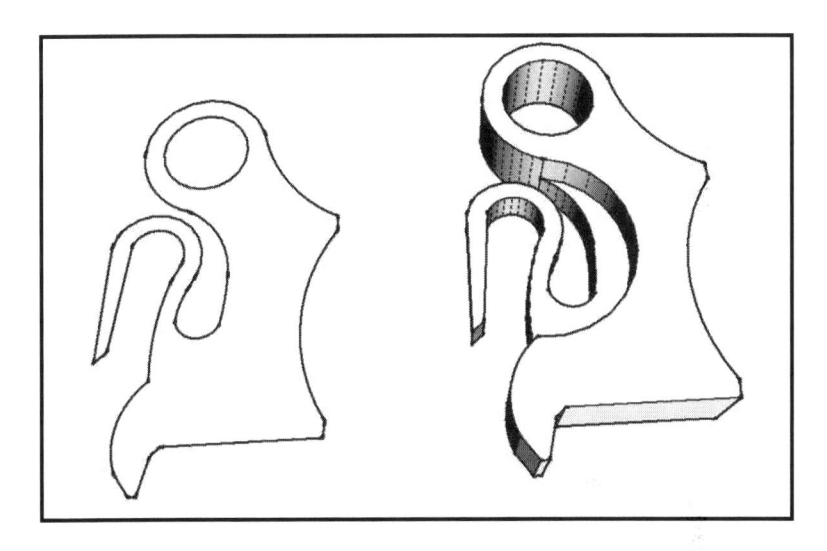

Drawing a 2d shape using the measurements taken from the cardboard template and handle, the part is then "extruded" up to make a 3D prism of the desired shape. Details such as the partial height of the spring shown here can then be added prior to finalizing the design. (Illustration by author)

Because I was printing a spring, I used 1.5mm wall (perimeter) thickness.

Springs tend to work better when they are solid or nearly so, and the best way to fill them in is by increasing the perimeter thickness rather than setting the infill to 100%. This is because the orientation of the extrusion lines will be in line with the spring shape when perimeters are printed, but not (necessarily) when infill is printed.

A quick look at the tool path verifies that the return spring will print as a near solid, for maximum resilience and durability. (Illustration by author)

It is often useful to incorporate functional details such as springs into parts like this one. The "trick" to plastic springs is to make the spring as long as possible, so that the deflection is spread over a large area. This way, the stresses from bending are well distributed, and the elasticity of the plastic can return the part to its original shape without permanent deformation.

For a more in depth and technical study of plastic springs, latches, hinges, and other design details for 3D printing beyond what is found in this book, take a look at the book *Functional design for 3d printing*, available online or at your local bookseller through Ingram or Baker & Taylor publishers.

After printing, I tested the spring through its entire range of motion and then some, looking for evidence of stress failure. This can be seen on ABS parts as tiny white lines that form on the surface of the print where most of the stretching is taking place. After seeing none, I intentionally overstressed the spring to see where and when stress fractures would appear.

Satisfied that extreme excursions from design conditions were necessary to produce stress fractures in the spring, and that even after over-stressing, the spring still functioned as intended, I printed another part for actual installation.

I installed the part and tested it through its range of motion, checking for looseness, stickiness, reliable operation, and general ergonomic usability. No problems were found or changes indicated, so I assembled the saw and cut some wood as a test.

I have used a similar process to repair many items, and even for complex parts a cardboard or thin plastic cut-out template can be very useful as a starting point.

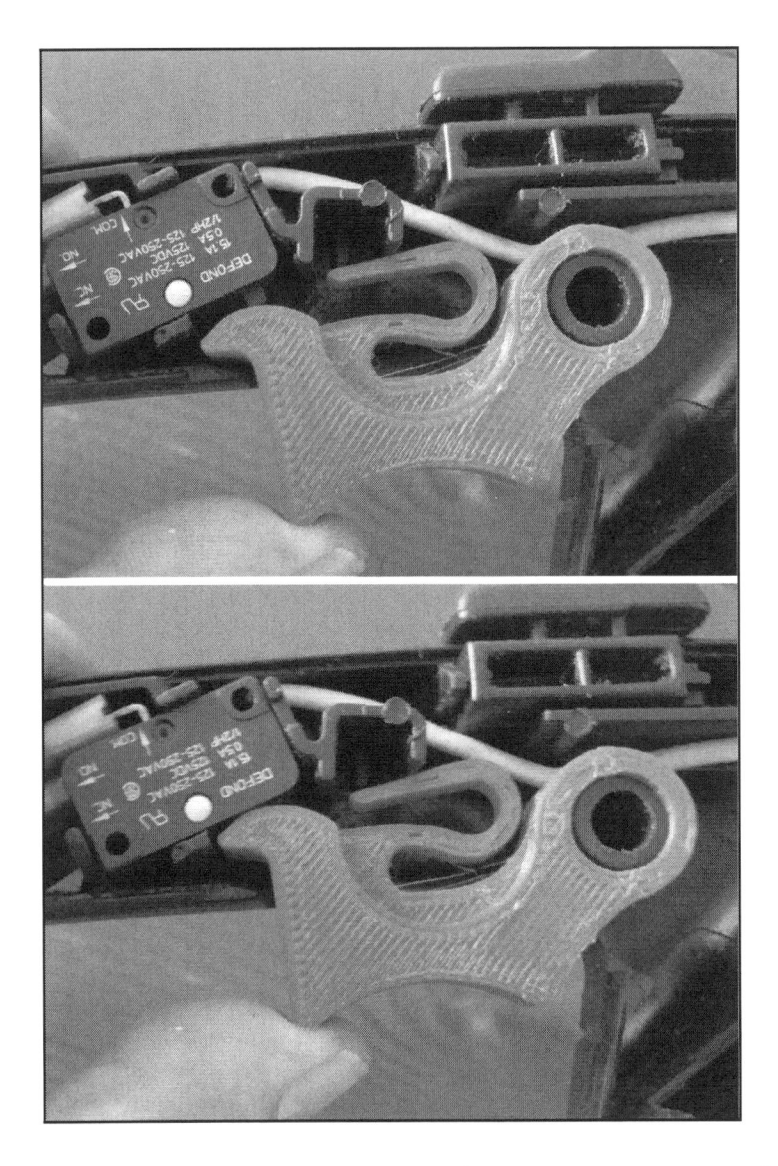

Test fitting and function testing of the new trigger. Note the long span and minimal deflection of the spring during activation. This will insure that the spring does not fail from fatigue over its expected lifetime. (Photo by author)

71

Test pieces can often be printed to a minimal height and checked, and then the "real" part printed after finalizing the design. Nozzle overloading allows fast turnaround for prototypes (or even finished parts), and enables you to get results much faster than printing at regular settings.

The completed part, installed for final inspection and function testing. (Photo by author)

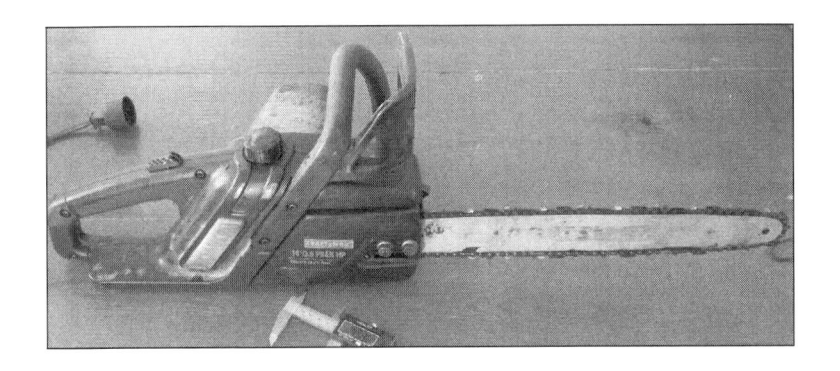

A few minutes and a 3D printer turned this chainsaw from a pile of parts into a useful tool. (Photo by author)

Next time you have something that could be fixed if you just had a new piece, try these simple, easy to apply techniques to streamline your prototyping workflow.

Chapter 3

Making it fit: Hinges, latches, and joinery.

Often it is necessary to include functional elements like hinges, latches, or joints into your print. In this chapter, we will discuss some examples of functional elements that can be easily adapted to your needs. Although typically no match for their metal counterparts, you won't have to go scavenging into infected territory to come up with these, and they can often be made integral to your designs. Despite being made out of plastic, engineered features can be surprisingly strong when properly designed - especially when printed from high strength plastics and nylons.

Another critical survival skill for 3D printing is building large items, and this is often improved when the objects can interlock. Printing interlocking structures to join parts of large or small objects can make assembly quick and accurate, and can eliminate scrounging in dangerous grocery or hardware stores for overlooked superglue.

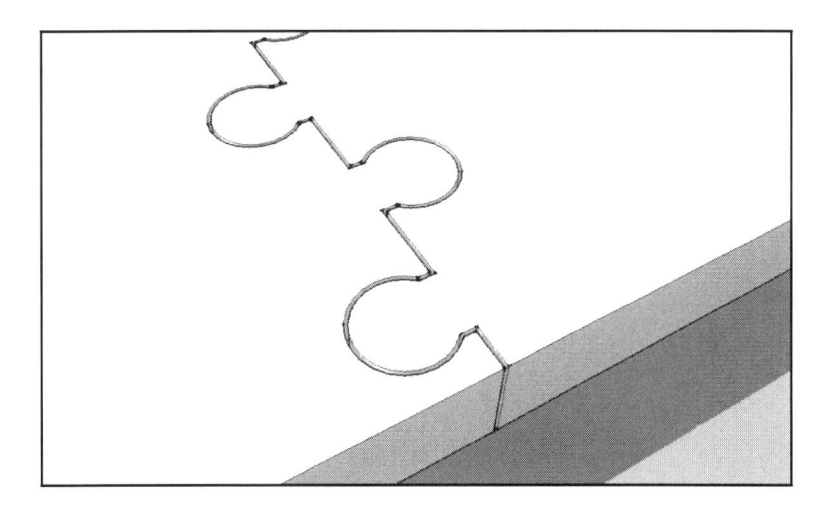

An example of interlocking "puzzle edges". Using this or similar forms, items larger than the build area of the printer can be assembled from separate parts while maintaining perfect alignment and good structural integrity. In most cases, these types of interlocks should be printed flat on the bed. (Illustration by author)

Often, assemblies can be built so that they fit together and are held in place by an external ring or retaining structure. This is especially useful in cases like the tripod depicted in the following illustration, though it can be applied any time that parts need to be tightly bundled together.

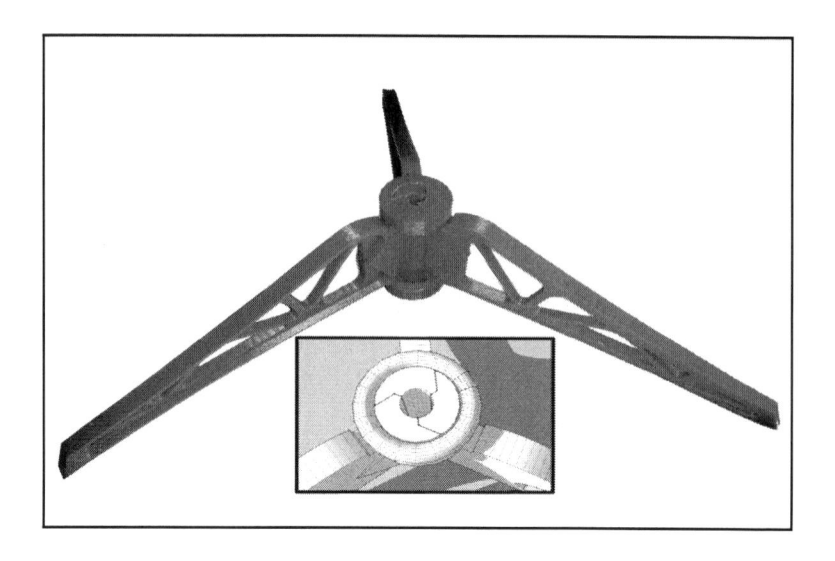

450MM (18") Printed tripod base. Each of the legs are printed separately, flat on the print bed, and fit together in the center forming a tube. The tube is pressed into printed rings top and bottom. The assembly is rigid and strong, requiring no non-printed parts or glue. (Photo by author)

Dovetail or sliding type joints are very useful when multiple parts must be joined together in intersecting planes, especially when one piece needs to be oriented differently than another to give it the required strength. In many cases, inspiration for the application of this type of joint is usefully derived from things made out of wood, as the anisotropic similarities of wood and FFM structures lead to similar functional solutions.

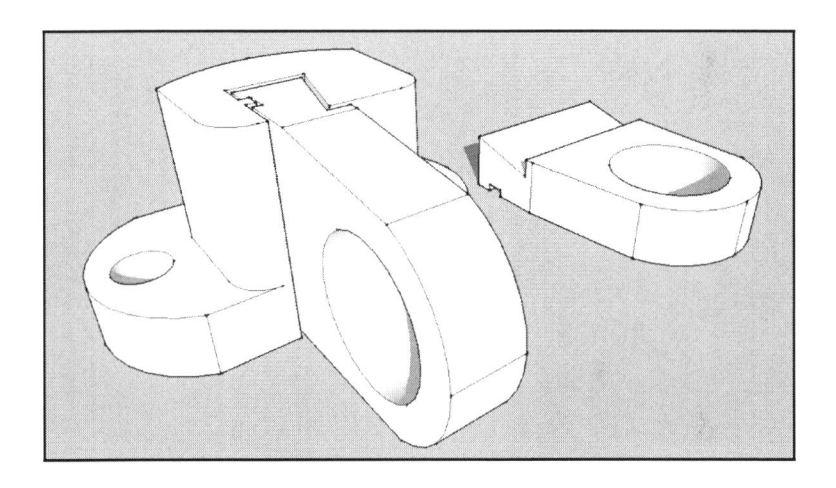

A modified dovetail joint designed for the tongue to be printed lying flat. This allows the anisotropic (grain wise) strength properties to be optimized for load bearing in two different directions in the assembled piece. If printed in one piece, the load bearing eye would be relatively fragile and would not support significant loading. (Illustration by author)

Dovetail joints should be designed with a little bit of extra clearance, and given extra room at any corners in the joint pocket.

With few exceptions, strength is critical in engineered features. Flexing parts must be oriented so that any flexing occurs in the X-Y plane, and little or no flexibility is required in the Z direction. For example, the latches shown in the illustrations that follow must be printed flat as drawn.

Parts that flex on the z axis are unlikely to be strong enough to provide reliable service. In contrast, joinery such as dovetail joints and interlocking structures (especially the sockets from these structures, which are subjected to tensile loads) work better when printed along the Z axis, as the X-Y strength will keep the "female" part of the joint from opening or cracking. The "male" part in can be printed in either orientation, but not oriented so that the protrusion goes from the base to the tip on the Z-Axis. This aspect of dovetail type joints makes them very useful when the direction of strength must be varied.

An important thing to remember when designing these kinds of features is that in a properly calibrated printer, parts will normally come out slightly oversized due to overextrusion. *Proper calibration will not remove this variation.* The reasons for this are discussed in detail in the section on printer calibration in chapter 4.

To compensate for the size increase caused by overextrusion, the model must be designed slightly smaller than the desired part. The overextrusion allowance will vary with printing conditions, but using ½ of the nozzle width setting is a good starting point.

For example:

- If printing with a 0.4mm nozzle width setting, allow 0.2mm of overextrusion in designs.

- If a 6mm fastener needs to fit snugly through a hole, design the hole to be 6.4mm in diameter – 0.2mm on each side of the hole for overextrusion allowance.

- If a part must have an edge precisely 37mm from the center of a hole, design the part to extend 36.8mm from the centerline of the hole, allowing 0.2mm for overextrusion along that edge.

- If designing an alignment peg on one part to fit into another printed part, make the socket 0.8mm larger than the peg, allowing 0.2mm x2 for the sides of the socket, and 0.2mm x2 for the sides of the peg.

- If fitting a hole for a preexisting peg, only allow peg diameter + 0.2mm x2, because the physical peg is measured at actual size in this case.

In practice, the ½ nozzle width allowance may too much or too little. Overextrusion will vary based on print speed, material being printed, layer height, filament variations, water content of filament, etc.

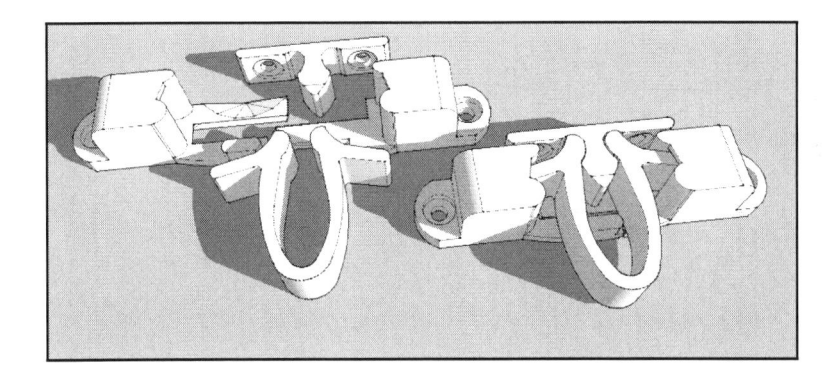

A printed cabinet latch. This latch is assembled by sliding the two halves together over the gripper spring, and is held together by the screws used to mount the latch to the cabinet. Proper part tolerances designed into the model allow easy, snug assembly with little or no post print processing. (Illustration by author)

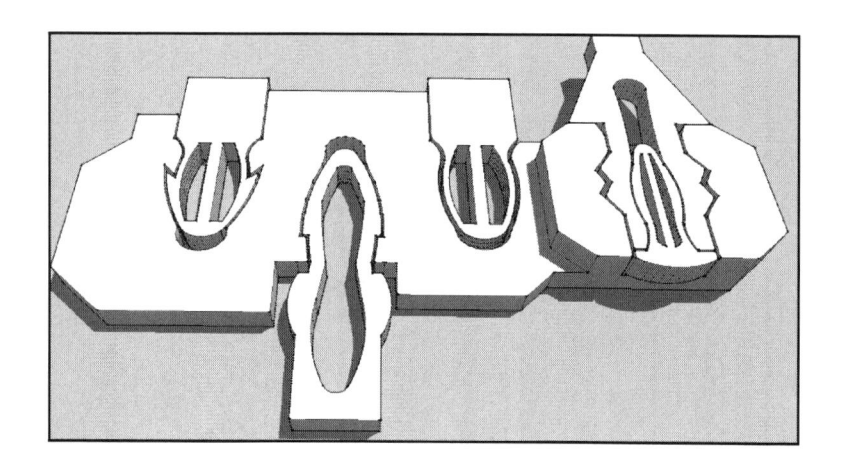

A variety of snap-fit fastening techniques, some permanent and some removable. Note the pocket at the tip of each inserted part to allow enough over-insertion for the latching mechanism to snap into place. Note how the flexing elements are designed to be printed flat, with thin sections designed to allow limited flexibility. The examples are designed to be printed in ABS, PET, or a harder nylon such as Taulman 910. Some PLA blends may also produce suitable results. Variations of these designs can be used to make latches, fasteners, and to secure parts together. (Functional design for 3d printing)

When using a nozzle width setting wider than your actual nozzle width (nozzle overloading) and tall layers, overextrusion can go up to about 0.8 of the nozzle width setting with some filaments, and can exceed the actual nozzle diameter. The best way to be sure is to print the parts and test fit them.

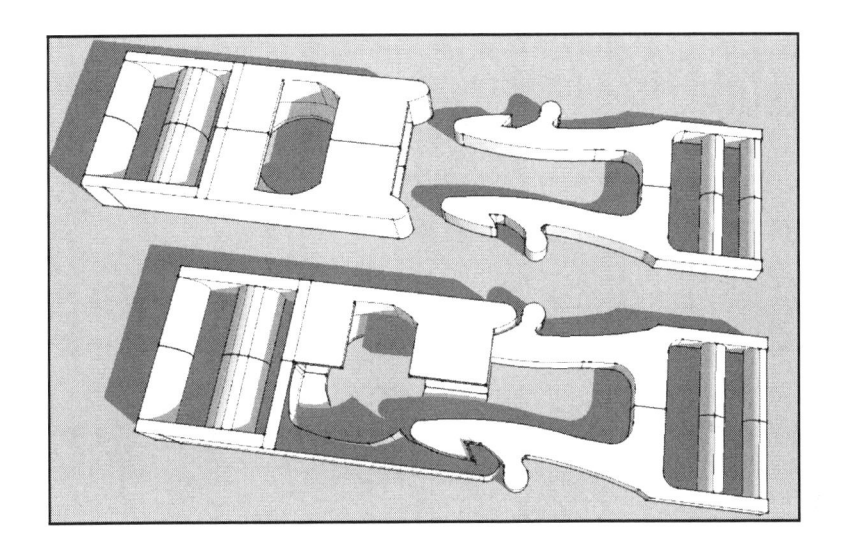

A snap fit buckle. Remember that objects like latches and buckles often require some flexibility to function. It is important to choose a slightly flexible filament and print these structures flat on the bed (X-Y as shown) to achieve a satisfactory outcome. In tests, buckles similar to this one can support over 50 KG when properly proportioned and printed. (Illustration by author)

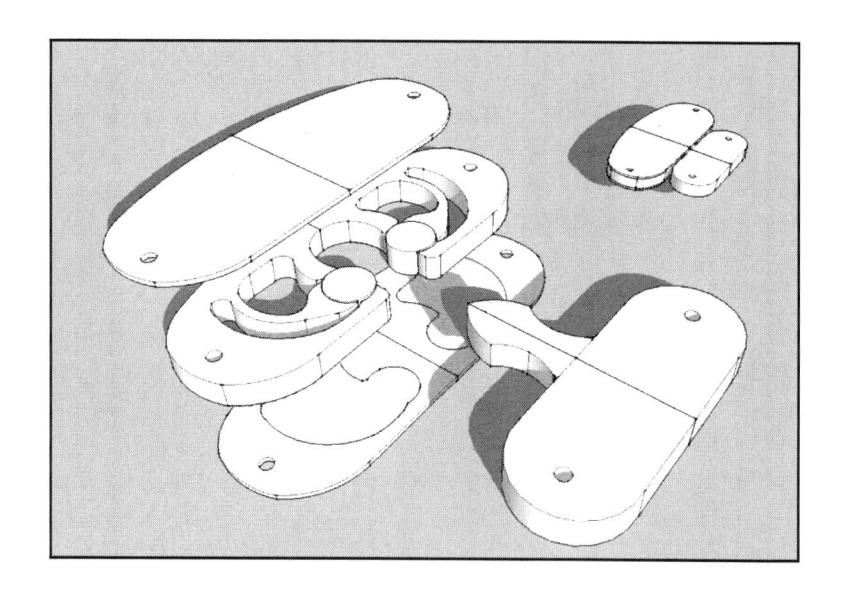

A more sophisticated cabinet / box latch. This latch features rollers that facilitate a smooth locking and releasing action. Note the recesses on the cover plates to allow unimpeded motion for the rollers and the spring-arms. (Illustration by author)

Hinges:

Hinges are generally of two types. The simplest type, the living hinge, relies on the flexibility of the printed material.

Living hinges work well in some ABS and flexible PLA plastics, and are excellent in nylons, PET, and TPU filaments.

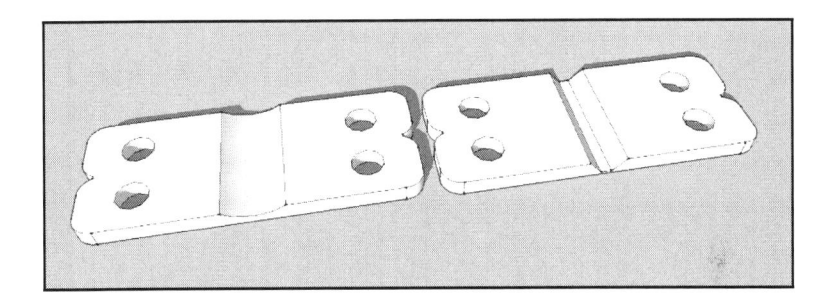

Living hinges. The hinge on the left is optimized for flexible materials like soft nylons and elastomeric plastics, while the type on the right is preferred for less flexible nylons, ABS, PET, and similar materials.(Illustration by author)

For repeated use, living hinges must be printed from flexible materials like nylon or TPU. PLA and ABS, especially more flexible varieties, work well for limited use. This can be especially handy for parts that are hinged only to aid the assembly process, like glider wings that pivot up to their final position for assembly while maintaining alignment with the fuselage.

Living hinges should be 0.3mm to 1.5mm thick (around 0.5mm-1mm for ABS), and should be a minimum of two layers when printed.

The web, or bending part, should typically be designed 1.5mm wide or more, (at least 4 times the web thickness) and should have a bit of slack when in the extended position for repeated use. The parts leading up to the hinge should be tapered to allow the hinge to move without binding.

"Pin and barrel" hinges (like a standard door hinge) can be made in many variations using both plastic or wire / bolt / nail pins, but I find that for most applications, a superior hinge can be made using a metallic pin. Using a plastic pin is possible of course, but this increases the size of the hinge considerably to achieve similar strength, and the pins typically do not provide the kind of service life you might get from a metal pin in any case. Pin and barrel hinges provide good service in ABS or PLA, and are exceptionally durable in PET or Nylon filaments.

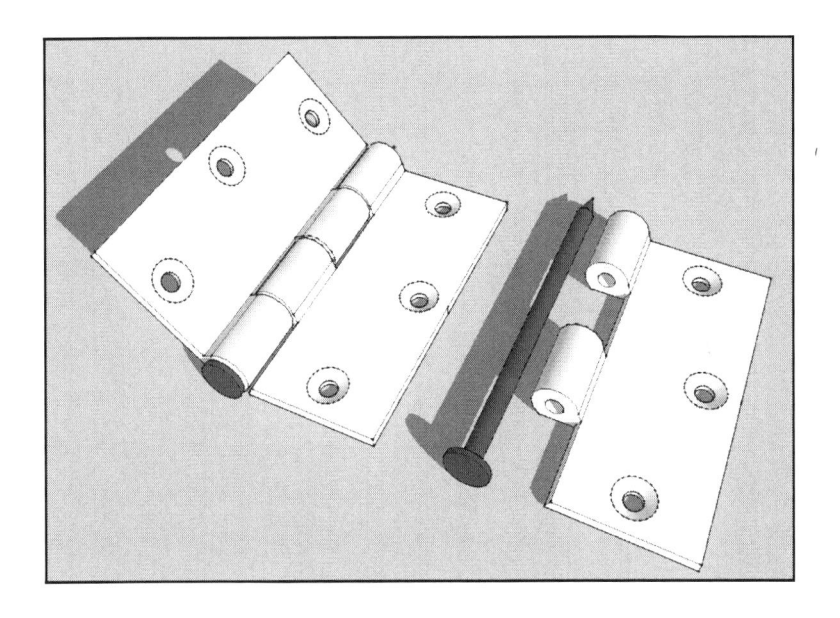

A conventional pin and barrel hinge, optimized for harder nylons. This design uses a common steel nail as a hinge pin, eliminating the need for printing this critical part. In ABS or PLA this design works well for light duty use such as boxes and cupboards. In high strength nylon, this part has provided excellent long term service for lightweight interior doors. (Illustration by author)

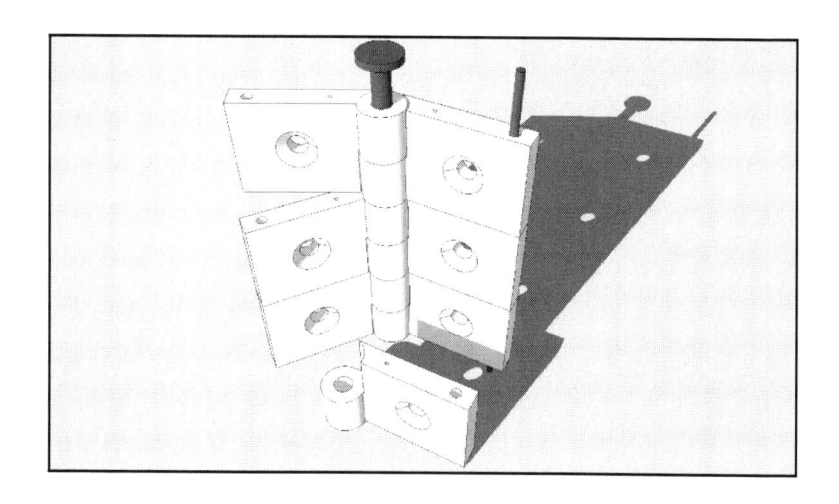

An "infinite" pin and barrel hinge, designed to give durable service even in ABS or PLA. Note the extendable design, the reinforcing holes, and the ability to use wire at the outer hole to provide additional integrity. (Illustration by author)

Making it springy:

Both ABS and PLA can be used to print suitable springs for many applications, with ABS being slightly more durable and less brittle than most PLA formulations. PET and nylon deliver superior service life, with PET being a little more rigid and nylon more resistant to fatigue stress.

TPU or similar "rubber" filaments can be used to print band type elastic springs, shock absorbing structures, and "bumper" stops, but are rarely rigid enough for entire assemblies.

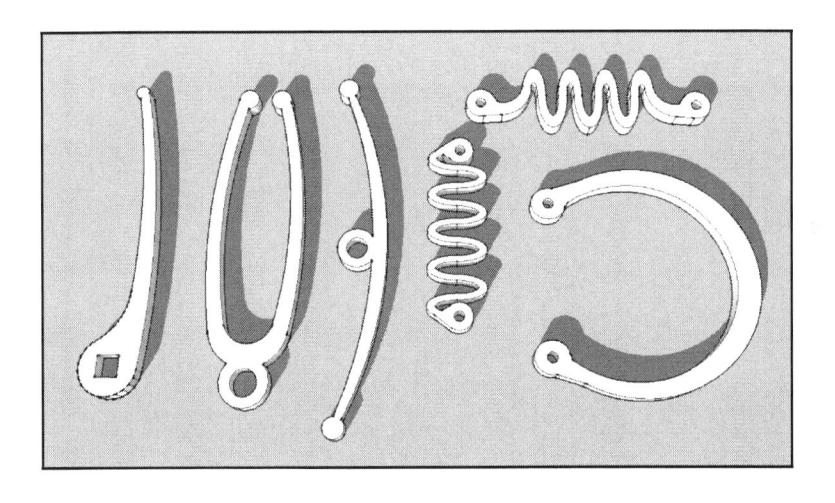

Some examples of printed spring design. Depending on the application, springs can be printed from most plastics though their characteristics will vary widely between materials. With few exceptions, springs should be printed flat in the X-Y plane as shown for best durability. These springs were successfully used in different mechanisms, all printed in ABS. (Illustration by author)

By using multiple materials together, such TPU with PET or ABS, rigid structures with flexible elements can be built either using a dual extrusion printer, or by printing the parts separately and assembling them post-printing.

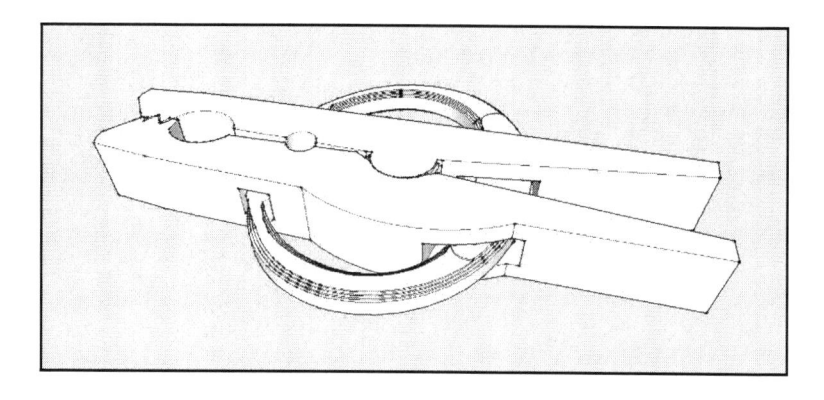

A printable clothespin with a c-spring, for printing in ABS. The spring and the two halves are printed separately and assembled as shown. This design has shown similar utility to standard wooden clothespins. (Illustration by author)

Using "vitamins"

Although it is sometimes desirable to build things completely from printed parts or even in one printed piece, the most useful objects are frequently made with the addition of "vitamins", or commonly available standard parts. These easily available bits of hardware can multiply the utility of your print while adding relatively little to the cost.

An excellent example of this principle can be found in the opensource printer revolution itself. Using off the shelf electronic components and stuff you can source from any good hardware store, a complex, high precision Cartesian factory robot can be constructed with minimal skill from printed parts and no need for expensive machining or sophisticated tools.

If you think about it, a high precision industrial robot isn't exactly the simplest or even the most obvious application for 3D printing, so considering what other items could be made instead of purchased using the "vitamin rich" approach might prove to be a fruitful endeavor.

A C-clamp alongside its printed components. With the addition of a 6mm (or ¼") bolt and a couple of nuts, these easily printed parts become a very useful tool. While it is certainly possible to print a C-clamp without using any "vitamins", the print would need to be much more complex and bulky to achieve the same utility and strength. (Illustration by author)

Using the high strength and precision of steel screws, bolts, and other parts can open up a whole new world of possibilities as you channel their properties into useful objects using 3D printing.

With the addition of a few machine screws, a bolt, and a couple of skate board bearings, a 4 inch (100mm) pulley that will safely support well over 100 kilos can be printed. This would be very difficult to do without the few bits of hardware used, although probably the only absolutely essential part of this design is the axle bolt. The other screws and the bearings help to make it a durable, serviceable item that will stand up to everyday use. (Illustration by author)

Thermoforming

Thermoforming refers to the process of heating and shaping a part, then allowing it to cool in the desired form. Once cool, it will typically retain its new shape.

Since FFM printing processes use thermoplastics almost exclusively, most FFM printed parts can be thermoformed rather easily. Perhaps one of the most common examples of thermoforming a 3D printed part is to heat a screw or bolt before screwing it into a hole on a print, creating thermoformed threads.

In some cases, it can even be useful to thermoform filament directly, without even printing it first. A good example of this is making coil springs by winding heated filament around an armature.

To thermoform a plastic, it must be heated above its glass transition floor. This temperature varies from plastic to plastic, but for many ABS compounds it is around 110°C, and for PLA it is about 65°C.

PLA is particularly well suited to thermoforming. It has a low thermoforming temperature (80-100°C) which is easily achieved by immersion in boiling water. It has a wide temperature range between excellent plasticity and melting, and has a useful tendency to "remember" its original shape and return to it when heated.

Because of printed PLA's tendency to recover its original form when reheated after thermoforming, it can also be used to make "heat shrink" assemblies. To do this, a printed part is heated, then stretched or otherwise deformed and allowed to cool. The thermoformed part is then installed and reheated, where it recovers its original form. This could be useful in making clamping hose retainers, for example, which can be set by inserting the assembly into hot water. In this case the pre-expanded clamp would shrink - securing the hose - much like heat-shrink tubing. Heat shrinking bands have a variety of applications where a tight fit is needed, especially on an irregular surface.

This shape memory characteristic might also prove useful for "ship in a bottle" applications, where a large part could be inserted in a collapsed or folded form through a small orifice, before being returned to its original shape by reheating. This principle could be useful for fasteners, as well as structures requiring tension to achieve desired structural characteristics.

Chapter 4

Getting the most out of your printer

This is not meant to be an exhaustive treatise on print troubleshooting, but rather an introduction to some of the most common issues, their causes, and remedies. Each printer type has its own idiosyncrasies, and your best troubleshooting resources will probably be the user community and forums for your particular printer design.

The first layer of print quality

Often, a print succeeds or fails based on the integrity of the first layer. If the first layer adheres well, the print will progress unless a major failure of some kind occurs. It the first layer does not adhere to the bed, the print will deform, curl, or even come loose from the bed completely and printing will fail.

A good first layer should be firmly attached to the bed and a little bit squashed, but not so squashed that surplus plastic leaves troublesome ribbon like artifacts or lumps. The first layer nozzle height must be high enough to allow clean extrusion, but not so high that the plastic is left just laying on the bed without bonding tightly to adjacent extrusions and the printing surface. A proper first layer will be high enough to create a strong structural base and level out minor bed imperfections, but not so high that the edges of the print become poorly defined or imprecise.

In order to achieve good first layer printing, a few things have to be in order. First, the bed must be level with the X and Y axes. Many printers incorporate automatic bed leveling features that compensate for unlevel beds, but you will achieve the best results if you manually level the bed as a starting point for automatic compensation. Second, the bed must be relatively flat, without significant warping or defects. The better bed leveling algorithms can compensate for a slightly warped bed, but even in the best case, a non–flat bed means non-flat prints. Lastly, the Z axis zero point (home) must be accurately set.

The Z-home setting is the reference point where the print nozzle is barely touching the print bed. This setting must be correct to achieve good first layer results.

When the Z-home setting is correct, a smooth, solid first layer will result if printed using the appropriate information for filament diameter and composition on a well calibrated printer. A slight change in starting height (dependent on the Z-home adjustment) can make a big difference. A few hundredths of a millimeter too high, and a poorly adhered, sieve like first layer will be printed. Just a little too low, and a rough surface with globs and ribbon artifacts will result. Automatic bed leveling software can also provide automatic Z-homing on some printers, which can make things easier.

This photo shows a poorly adhered, stringy first layer. Note the lack of bonding between lines and to the perimeter at the outer edges. A first layer like this can lead to detachment of the print from the bed, and subsequently to total print failure. There is little or no flattening of the extrusion, due to the distance from the bed as the plastic is extruded. This problem is usually caused by an excessively far Z-home setting, but can also result from a low spot on an unlevel bed, or extrusion problems like filament drive slippage. (Photo by author)

If the Z-home is not correct, the print may try to start in mid air, suffer poor adhesion, or the extruder may scrape forcefully on the bed.

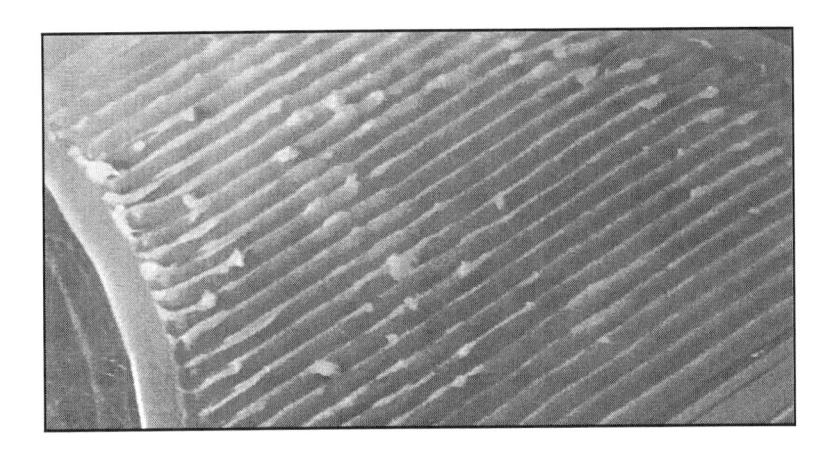

This photo shows a rough, gouged first layer. Note the grooves in the extrusion where the fill lines meet the perimeter, and the ribbon like extrusion artifacts on the print. This is caused by a too-close Z-home setting or a high spot on an unlevel bed. The ribbon artifacts can drag on the head while printing the next layer, causing positioning errors and globbing that can lead to print failure. Moving the Z-home distance slightly away from the bed should correct this issue. (Photo by author)

Before adjusting the Z-Home or bed leveling, the Z-mechanism may need to be checked for synchronization. This is the case if your printer uses a separate drive for each side of the Z axis, as in most MENDEL based printers (Prusa, i3, etc). This can be accomplished by measuring the height of the X- axis carriage from the *frame* of the printer (not the bed) on both ends, and adjusting the lead screws so that both sides are equal. If this frequently gets out of adjustment, you may have a stepper driver adjustment issue or excessive friction in one side or the other of the Z-drive.

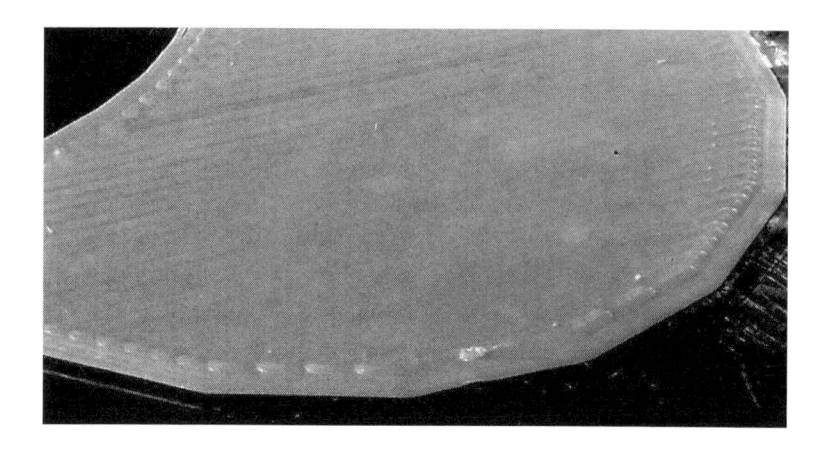

This photo shows a well adhered, relatively smooth first layer. Note the complete bonding between fill lines and the perimeter at the outer edges. There is uniform flattening of the extrusion, and no curling artifacts. The small artifact in the foreground will not pose any problem for the next layer (Photo by author)

An approximate adjustment of the Z-height can be achieved with a piece of regular printer paper. First, preheat the extruder to operating temperature. While maintaining this temperature (and a working bed temperature as well, if desired), place the paper on the print bed, and adjust the Z- home height until there is slight friction from the nozzle when moving the paper. Repeat at all corners and the center of the bed to check for proper leveling and flatness. Ideally, the paper should have the same friction at all test points. Adjust the bed until any variations are minimized.

It can be time consuming, but fine tuning your printer and printing parameters to fabricate a smooth, well adhered first layer not only improves the reliability of your printing workflow, if also opens up a whole set of manufacturing options for high flexibility and membrane structures.

Bed adhesion

Even if the bed is properly adjusted, steps must often be taken to ensure that the print adheres to the bed during the printing process, but isn't stuck so thoroughly that it is difficult to remove without damage. The way this is achieved can vary greatly with the bed surface, the plastic being printed, and personal preference.

Design factors that influence bed adhesion are primarily related to the contact surface area of the print on the bed, and the tendency of the print to warp or pull away from the bed.

One of the greatest difficulties of printing large parts with materials that have significant thermal contraction while cooling (like ABS and Nylon) is warping. Warping is caused by the shrinkage of layers as they cool causing tensile stresses that pull the upper parts of the print together, causing the corners and edges to lift from the bed.

Because of this, large solids with significant (over 10mm) Z-height are particularly prone to curling and warping issues. Skeletonization or minimization of the cross section of the design as it goes up in the Z-axis can help to alleviate these stresses.

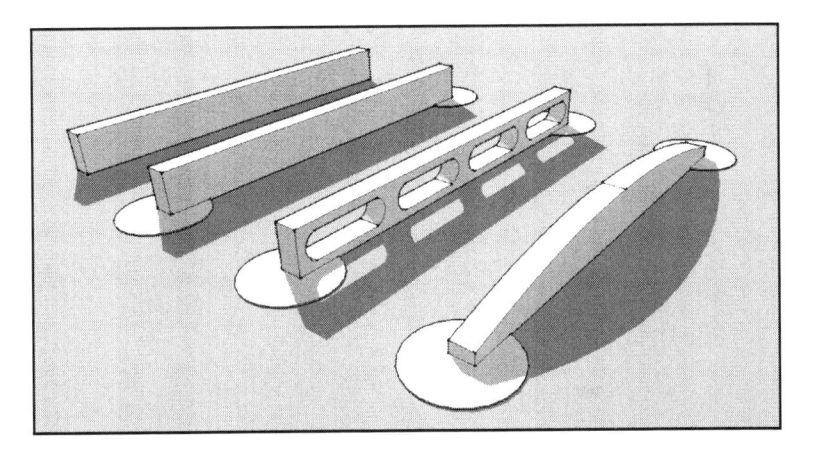

Four forms of a beam. The leftmost will likely suffer from warping when printed in high shrinkage plastic such as ABS or nylon. To the right are examples of adhesion pads, skeletonized structure, and minimizing structure endpoints in height – all effective methods to reduce warping and improve bed adhesion. (Illustration by author)

Design features such as contact pads or brims can be incorporated to increase the bed contact surface in critical areas, making the part less likely to lift from the bed while printing.

In most slicers, an automatically generated brim may be specified in the settings. Often this is all that is required, especially for small parts that are easily dislodged by the print head.

When other methods fail, a "raft" may be printed, creating a well-adhered first layer platform on which to build the print. This is an option in most slicing software, or it could be manually designed in the model if needed. Both rafts and brims must be removed during post print processing.

A heated printing surface and / or enclosure is often used to facilitate adhesion and minimize warping. When using materials like ABS or nylon that shrink a lot when cooling, the use of layer fans should be minimized, as cooling the upper layers of the print can exacerbate warping tendencies. Sometimes, this means that per-layer printing times must be increased to allow "natural" cooling of the print before the next layer is applied.

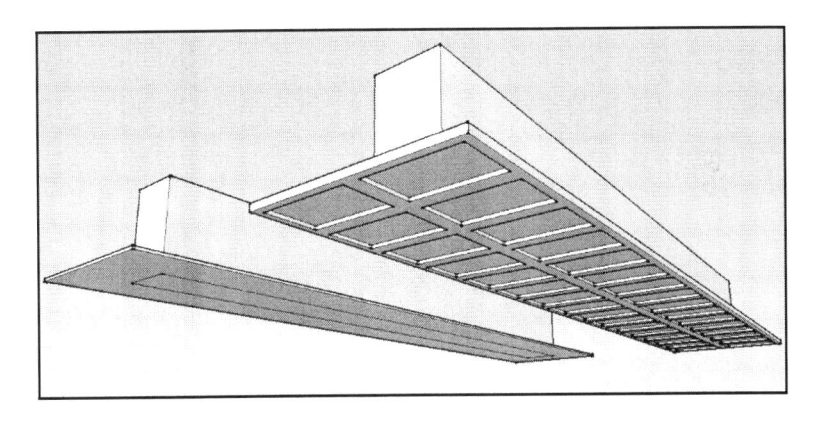

Underside of two beams. Leftmost beam includes a "brim" structure, effectively increasing the contact area of the bottom of the part. On the right, the beam is built on top of a raft structure which spreads out the warping stresses more effectively than the "brim" technique, but consumes more plastic and printing time. The "brim" removes easily, with minimal cleanup required, but rafts can sometimes require sanding or other cleanup of the bottom surface of the part. Both rafts and brims can be generated by most slicing software. (Illustration by author)

PLA does not usually warp or pull away from the bed as much as other plastics, so it is often printed on a plain glass bed, or on a printing surface such as Kapton or painters tape without the need for any bed-adhesion enhancing design features.

ABS is a little more troublesome, but works well on glass or Kapton using hairspray or a thin solution of ABS dissolved in PVC-ABS tubing cleaner or acetone.

Nylon is a little more difficult to stick to the bed, but does well on a melamine surface, or using PVA adhesive on a non-smooth surface such as blue painters tape.

PET (PETG) extrudes fairly well on glass or Kapton with PVA glue stick. Elmer's purple glue stick works well if you can find some still laying around. PVA glue sticks will be found in stationary and craft stores provided not too many people have gone looting for hallmark after the big chill.

Specialty filament suppliers usually have some guidance on the best surfaces or bonding agents for adhesion, as well as ideal temperatures and printing tips.

Calibration: This is going to get pretty technical.

Motion calibration of most 3D printers is a function of pulley size, screw or belt pitch, and the per step angular motion of the motors.

Generally, the stock settings for your factory printer will be pretty accurate. As a printer gets used however, the length between the teeth of the belt can vary slightly with changes in tension, or the original calibration might not have been that accurate to start with. I have seen some new out of the box printers with calibration errors as much as 3%.

In most cases the effects of a slight miscalibration are not even noticeable, but imprecise calibration can be problematic when you are trying to print something to precise dimensions.

Many references to printer calibration talk about printing a calibration cube or other object and examining / measuring it to achieve proper calibration. While this is a useful technique, it will result in suboptimal calibration for absolute accuracy. This is because of overextrusion.

Printed objects are always slightly larger than the outside edge of the outer perimeter as described by the print nozzle, because some plastic squeezes out slightly (overextrudes) to the unobstructed side. For example, if your printer has a 0.5mm print head, and your settings are properly adjusted to ensure good interlayer adhesion (not underextruding), then an upright 0.5mm wall will print slightly wider than 0.5mm. In fact, it will probably be closer to 0.6mm, a 20% increase in width!

Now, consider a 20mm calibration cube, printed on a properly calibrated printer. It should measure 20mm on a side, right? Nope. It will measure 20mm + 0.2mm to 0.4mm. This is because of overextrusion at the edges. Now, you might ask…why not just calibrate out the error? So, let's do that. A 20.4 mm cube for a 20.0mm part represents a roughly 2% error, so we dial down our X and Y axes by 2%. Now the 20mm cube prints at exactly 20mm. Perfect, right?

Not unless you are only printing 20mm cubes.

Now take our newly calibrated printer that prints perfect 20mm cubes, and we print out a 100mm cube. The cube will come out at 98.4 mm on a side….Our error increased from 0.4mm to 1.6mm! What happened?

What happened is that we calibrated for printed part size, not for tool (print head) motion. Printed part size incorporates a fixed overextrusion error that is always a function of nozzle size. Tool motion errors are cumulative, and increase as a multiple of object size....so with different sized objects, the relationship between tool error and overextrusion error is non – linear, so you can't compensate for one by adjusting the other.

The point here is that while printing calibration objects is very useful for examining print quality and quantifying overextrusion allowances, it is not a good way to calibrate the absolute motion of your printer.

Most printers use "e-steps" or a similar parameter to describe the number of (micro) steps that a servomotor must move to achieve 1 unit (1mm usually) of motion. Adjusting this parameter is a procedure that varies wildly between printers, and you must know how to do this in order to calibrate your printer. It may be an option available of the printer menu itself, it may be in your desktop control software, or it may require manually tweaking, compiling, and reloading the printer firmware. Read the documentation pertaining to your printer for more information. If you don't know what you are doing, study the problem until you have a solid idea of how to proceed. Be advised that in some cases an incorrect setting change can cause something to actually catch on fire, though this normally pertains only to manual firmware changes.

If you know the relevant data about your printer, the following formula gives your e-steps exactly for belt driven axes: Esteps = (number of steps in a complete motor revolution * number of microsteps per step) / (number of teeth on the pulley * distance between teeth on the belt, or pitch, *in units used for Estep settings*). For screw type axes, it would be Esteps = (number of steps in a complete motor revolution * number of microsteps per step) / (distance between threads on the screw, or pitch, *in units used for Estep settings*) In practice, the threaded rod settings should always stay correct, but belts are subject to stretching which can change the effective pitch of the belt, though with good belts this effect is minimal.

If you are manually calibrating your printer, you will need to do the math after taking some measurements: To calculate new values for your "e-steps", take your commanded motion amount (say 100mm), and divide it by the actual measured motion (say 101.2mm) to get the e-step multiplier....in this case 0.98814292, or .9881 because 4 digit precision is sufficient. Multiply this by the current e-steps setting to get your new e-steps setting. Set the new e-steps setting in the printer, then "rinse and repeat" until you are confident that you are close enough.

To perform the measurements necessary to manually calibrate (or check) your X, Y, and Z axes, find a way to measure between a fixed point on your printer and a moving part of the axis being calibrated. This measurement must be taken precisely in alignment with the direction of motion. Set the axis being measured to one extreme of its motion. Take a measurement from a stationary part of the printer aligned with the direction of motion. Direct the printer to move the axis to nearly the other extreme of its motion and take another measurement form the same reference point. The idea is to measure how much it actually moves when you tell it to move a specific amount. Calibrate the printer motion settings based on these measurements (see the last paragraph for details) until you achieve repeatable, accurate movement by the printer. If you move the x axis 100mm in the controls, it should move as close to precisely 100mm as you can achieve. Do this for the X, Y, and Z axes.

Extruder calibration is a little trickier, because extruder drives always slip a little on the filament, and this slippage will vary based on print speed, filament material, and nozzle temperature, as well as a few other highly variable factors. The best strategy here is to simulate your most common printing conditions to get the best practical setting.

In a perfect world, you can measure the precise (linear) amount of filament consumed during a test print, and calibrate your extruder settings based on this until the actual filament used matches precisely the calculated (linear) filament that the print should use.

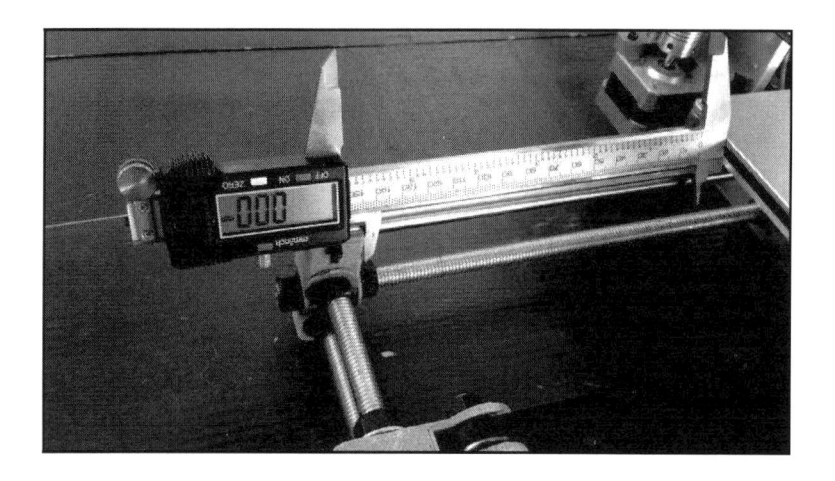

Measuring the Y Axis motion on a Prusa i3. The measuring instrument must be parallel with the axis motion. Accuracy is improved with longer travel measurements. (Photo by author)

The principal disadvantage to this is that you need to have software that will precisely tell you the number of millimeters of filament to be used, and not all software does this. It is best to have a number accurate to within 0.1mm, but even whole millimeters are sufficient if the test print consumes at least 200 mm of filament.

If measuring filament use in actual prints is not practical, a good approximation can usually be had by directly measuring filament throughput. Set up to print with your most common filament material / brand. Bring the nozzle to the normal printing temperature for that filament. Set the nozzle about 20mm off of the print bed. Trim the end of the filament to about 150mm from the extruder drive intake. Straighten the filament and measure how much is sticking out, within about 0.05mm. Order an extrusion of 100mm at the fastest extrusion speed that you normally use, and measure the remaining filament. Adjust extruder drive calibration until more or less precisely 100mm of filament is consumed.

This membrane print shows signs of underextrusion. With backlighting as shown, it can be seen that the print is lattice-like and not sealed, as it should be. (Photo by author)

This rough surface is caused by excessive moisture content in the filament, which creates steam bubbles during extrusion. (Photo by author)

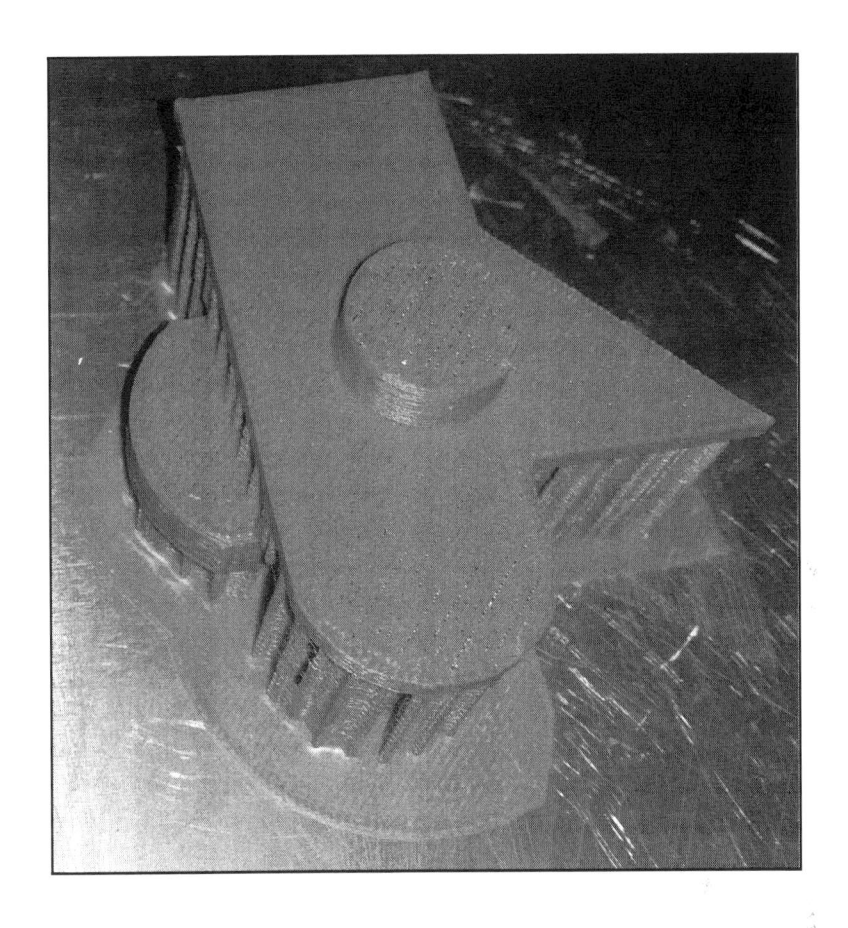

The top surface of this print shows underextrusion, as evidenced by the sieve like upper surfaces. Upper surfaces of two layers or more should be completely sealed. In this case, the filament size is probably slightly incorrect, but a slipping or poorly calibrated extruder could be the problem. (Photo by author)

This close-up photo of a print top layer shows clear signs of overextrusion. The layers below are overfilled, and there is not quite enough room to properly extrude the top layer. The symptoms are very similar to what is seen with a too – close Z-home adjustment, but are on the top surface of the print and are often accompanied by globbing and unevenness on the vertical structures. (Photo by author)

Here, a good second layer and one on a warped bed are contrasted. While the photo on the top shows a uniform sealed surface, the one on the bottom shows a region to the right where the layer adhesion is poor. Areas like this on your first or second layer are indications that the bed is out of level or warped. On some machines with two independent Z drives, it can also mean that the Z drives are out of synch. (Photos by author)

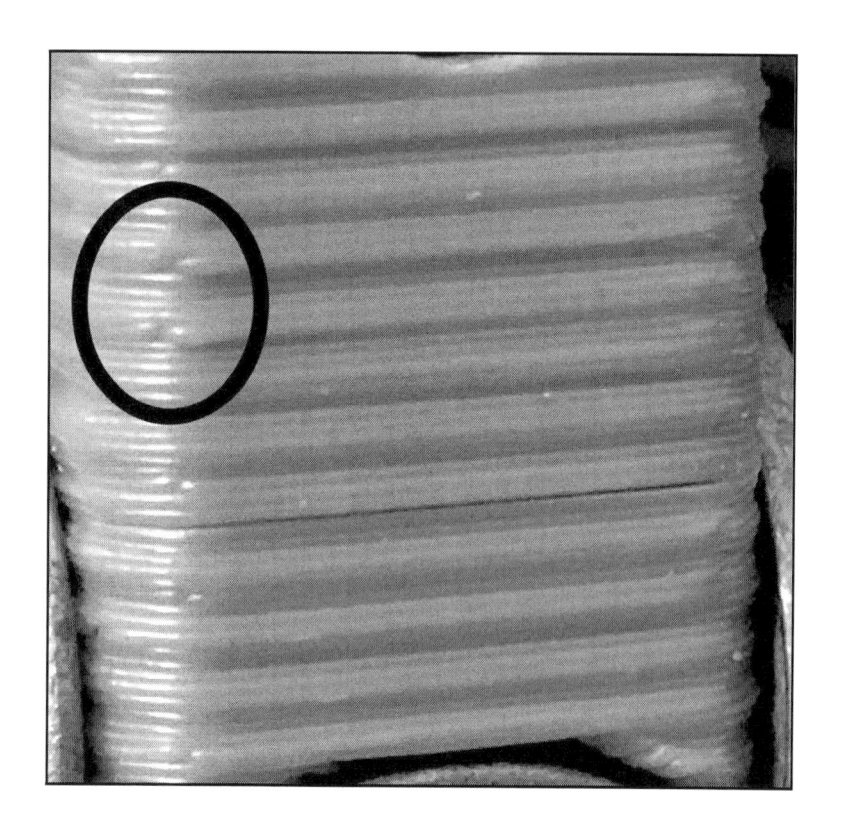

Periodic banding on the Z axis can be caused by crooked or off center Z drive screws, a layer height setting that is not a multiple of your per step motion, or sometimes by excessive looseness of belts, pulleys, or other parts. Here, the overlapping extrusions (inside circle) show evidence of belt looseness in the Y-Axis. The interlayer cracking shown here could be caused by excessive layer height, a slight underextrusion, low nozzle temperature, or thin walls with minimal infill on a poorly adjusted printer. (Photo by author)

Here, moisture saturated filament is extruded alongside dry filament. Notice the rough texture of the "foamy" filament. While generally regarded as a bad thing, the author has found that "foamy" extrusions are sometimes more shock resistant and less brittle than their prettier, non-foamy counterparts, although overall tensile strength suffers to some degree. (Photo by author)

Printing for Production: When printing one just isn't going to cut it.

When printed items are needed in bulk, optimizing your designs to print quickly can be important. Whether its antigen injectors, clothespins, or arrow fletchings - some things are better when you print more than one.

Printing in bulk brings additional scrutiny to print speed, reliability, and material efficiency. The general areas of emphasis in design optimization will be the same as optimizing for printability, but additional time investment in improving the design may be warranted for bulk items.

Anything that can be done to minimize the need for automatically generated support will likely prove worthwhile, and careful attention to rounding or clipping corners where possible can improve printing speeds and outcomes.

When printing multiple parts at once, visualizing the tool path can help to optimize the layout and check for any unnecessary complexity caused by the slicer. Here, visualization in CURA shows that there is little wasted motion in this layout. (Illustration by author)

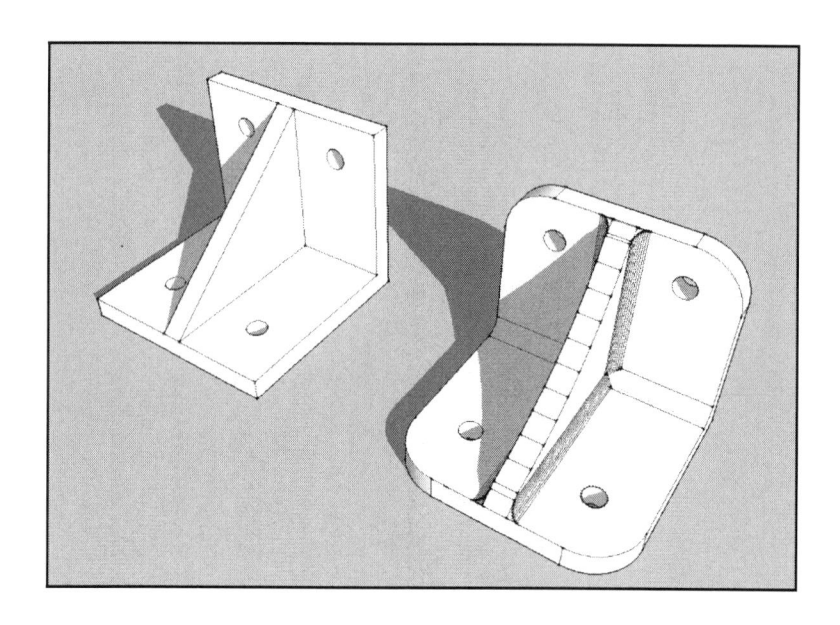

When possible, parts should incorporate curved edges and bevels. This helps to improve strength, while also improving printing speeds, print finish, and often reducing material use. In this example, the bracket on the right with the curved edges will consume slightly less plastic and print 33 seconds faster than the less durable one on the left. (Illustration by author)

Faster printing

Nothing is more frustrating than watching an antigen injector slowly rise from the build plate while your buddy goes into a drooling Z-factor stupor.

When speed is an important factor you can "super-size" your nozzle diameter up about 20% (30% for *cap'n, she can't take any more*' settings) from its actual diameter.

A 20% oversizing of your actual nozzle diameter along with a layer height of 75% (of your actual nozzle diameter) is the largest nozzle overload you will want to use in most applications. These settings will print items about twice as fast as "standard" settings (actual nozzle size and layer height of 50%) while still providing decent finish quality. This provides a much better result than just doubling the motion speed, which tends to cause print quality and reliability issues.

Keep in mind that when using this method (nozzle overloading) the allowance for overextrusion can go up quite a bit, especially when using tall layer heights. To ensure good fitting parts, test pieces should be printed at the desired production settings, and the design modified if needed to produce dimensionally acceptable prints. Nozzle overloading limitations will be bounded by the maximum extrusion speed for your extruder. Hot end wattage, extruder type, drive type, physical nozzle size, and filament composition are all factors in the maximum speed that can be achieved.

Another factor that affects print speed is sharp corners. At a sharp corner, the nozzle must slow to a near stop before changing direction. Although barely perceptible, this small increase in time can add up when compared to a part with rounded corners where the nozzle can continue at full speed. Due to the need for the print carriage to slow at sudden changes in direction, corners (in the X-Y plane at least) should be rounded wherever practical. This will reduce printing times and artifacts (blobbing) while improving the structural strength of most designs. Even where a rounded corner is impractical, a 45 degree clip of one millimeter or more at otherwise right angles can confer much of the speed and cosmetic benefit of a fully rounded corner.

Appendix I:

More case studies

Big, quick, and dirty:

A case study in printing larger items ASAP.

Aside from careful consideration and optimization of the design, changing the printing parameters to fit the use requirements can deliver big returns in speed and reliability, though often at the expense of an optimal surface finish.

In this project, I replaced a sewing machine pedal for which I only had most of the pedal top and the functioning base to work with. The required piece is roughly 90mm by 150mm, and needs to be pretty rugged to stand up to its usual use and abuse.

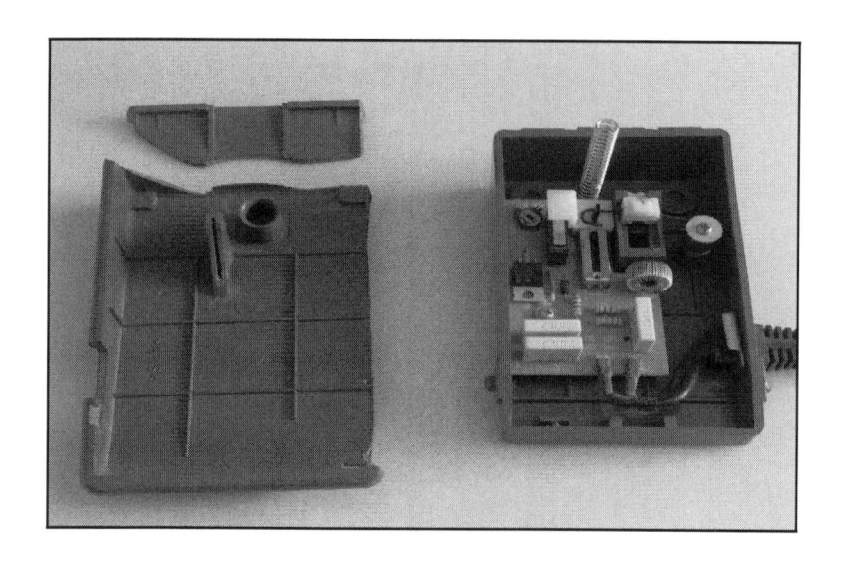

The broken sewing machine pedal. Since surface finish on this object is not important, I used it as an example of rapid production printing. (Photo by author)

For reasons of expediency, limited availability of electricity (I'm writing this in an area that has power available roughly 8 hours a day, usually at night), and just plain impatience, I decided to print the prototype piece as quickly as possible.

When increasing print speed, the first thing that tends to come to mind is dialing up the printing speed (mm/sec) parameters, but this is not really the best place to start. Increasing the motion speed is inherently limited by the maximum acceleration that the motors can provide, causes a lot of extra vibration, and often results in suboptimal extrusion. If the acceleration settings are not conservative enough in your firmware, high speeds can also result in skipped steps, ruining the print. Not only that, but chances are good that you are already doing most of your printing near the maximum practical speed of your printer, so dialing it up to "ludicrous speed" is likely to yield limited benefit in any case.

The most significant speed gains typically come both directly and indirectly from the nozzle diameter setting. This makes sense if you think about this in basic terms, because ultimately, the time it takes to build a print is much more closely tied to how fast you can extrude plastic onto the work surface than to the speed of the printhead.

You might be inclined to think "My nozzle is 0.35mm.... how am I supposed to change it?" That is a reasonable question, and the answer is "you could, but in this example, we won't." Instead of actually changing the nozzle diameter, we're going to take a more political approach, and just *say* that we did. This is called nozzle overloading.

As an example, my physical nozzle diameter is 0.4mm. For the sake of expediency, I frequently lie to my slicer and set the nozzle diameter setting to 0.5mm. While this slightly reduces fine feature definition, it doesn't affect resolution, per se. The x/y coordinates of the nozzle are defined by the minimum motor motion, not by the nozzle, so the nozzle size only limits the line width that can be extruded, not its positioning precision.

By saying that my nozzle is 0.5mm instead of the 0.4mm that it really is, I get a nearly free 25% speed gain. This works pretty well, because even though the hole in my nozzle is 0.4mm, the tip is considerably wider. Of course, when I need the best achievable fine feature definition, I use the actual 0.4mm width.

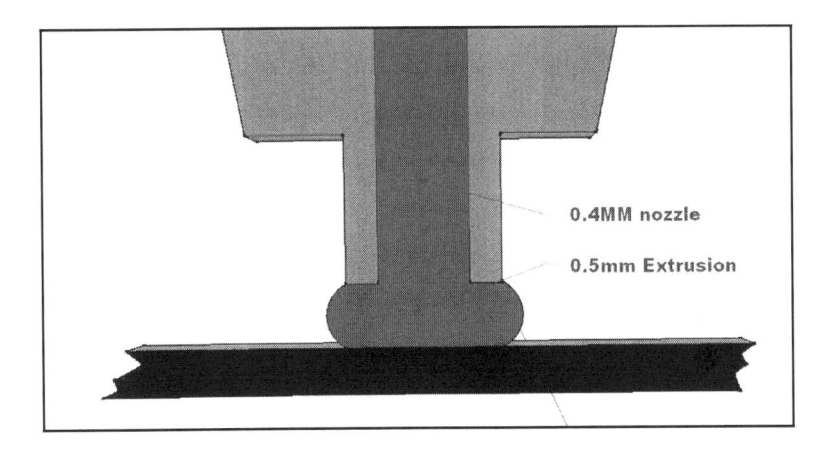

An example of "nozzle overloading". By setting the nozzle size in the slicer to a value up to 20% greater than the actual nozzle size, large gains in speed can be made with a minimal sacrifice in print quality in less finely detailed parts. Nozzle overloading will cause more overextrusion than normal print settings, so the dimensional allowances in the model may have to be adjusted to achieve an acceptable fit. (Illustration by author)

In addition to enabling wider line extrusions, wider nozzle width settings also enable thicker layers. Typically, layer heights up to 2/3 of nozzle width work well, so with a real nozzle width (0.4mm) I can go to 0.25mm with good interlayer adhesion, and with a fudged 0.5mm setting, 0.3mm layer heights work well. Using layer heights of 0.3mm and a nozzle width of 0.5mm, I can print the same object in 2/3 of the time it would take to print it at my maximum "real" settings, sacrificing surface finish, smoothness, and fine detail for speed. This is especially useful in utilitarian applications where surface finish is irrelevant and for prototyping where the part is probably going back to the shredder anyway.

In this particular case, I wasn't at all sure of the fit and function of my prototype drawing, and I didn't want to wait the 4 hour 24 minute nominal time to print with regular settings. Not only that, I don't give a whit about the finish on the pedal, and I can always sand it if it bothers me that much. I really wasn't happy with the idea of waiting 3 hours at the "politically inspired" settings either, so in this case I pulled out all the stops and went full FFM berserker mode.

A brief examination of the project reveals that the exposed exterior of the part is limited to the bed surface (which is nice and glossy flat regardless) and the exterior perimeter of a mostly straight surface. Even at very low fidelity settings, the mostly straight exterior should print nicely. All of the detail will be concealed inside and nothing is dimensionally critical in any case. This should be ideal for a case study in "quick and dirty" printability.

The ragged edge of "politically inspired 3D printing" is about 1.5x your actual nozzle diameter. For this case, that gives us a 0.6mm nozzle from our 0.4mm (real) nozzle. With a "0.6mm nozzle", we can print at a 0.4mm layer height. Pushing things to the maximum on both virtual nozzle width and layer height, I expect that interlayer adhesion will suffer a bit, but in this case the strength in Z-tension is non-critical. If layer adhesion proves to be problematic, the surface can be fused with PVC-ABS solvent or acetone which will make it much stronger with just a few minutes of post print processing.

Extruding at these settings will be 2.4 times as fast, so it would be logical to think that I should be able to print this out in 1 hour and 50 minutes, but in real life the gains are a little more, because fewer perimeters are needed to give the same wall thickness. This pushes more of the printing motion over to the faster infill process. This advantage will vary with the perimeter to area ratio of each layer, as well as the infill percentage. In this case, the print time for this item has been reduced from 4 hours 24 minutes to 1 hour 39 minutes, without changing any of the printing speed settings. In practice, I will tweak the print speed to 125%, picking up another ten minutes or so of time savings.

The limiting factor to this method is the maximum sustainable extrusion rate of your printer. This will vary with material type, and smooth printing plastics like ABS will yield better results than the typically more "sticky" ones like PLA.

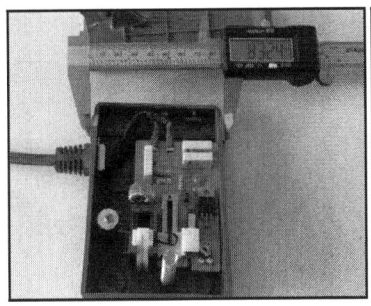

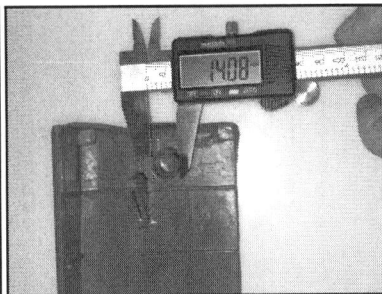

Careful measurement of the parts that must fit with your print is the important first step when building a replacement part. Don't forget to allow an overextrusion allowance on the edges of your model. Accuracy and attention to detail when working with critical dimensions will pay dividends in time and plastic saved. (Photo by author)

Extruder drive power and traction as well as hot end wattage can also be limiting factors.

Direct drive (non geared) extruders are typically more limited in the maximum extrusion rate, as are Bowden types due to additional friction in the tube. In his case, I am using a modified Wade's geared extruder with a directly attached 40 watt J-head. This simple setup is capable of printing relatively fast.

With a new printer, the best approach is to incrementally try increasing nozzle overloading until you start to get apparent extruder slippage or under-extruded structures. If you get to a nozzle width of 1.5x your actual nozzle and a layer height of 2/3 of the "fake" nozzle width, the practical maximum in most cases, it probably isn't worth going much further.

Printing at 0.6mm / 0.4mm, results were predictably rough, but acceptable in this case. The first prototype did have significant fitting issues caused by a surprising amount of overextrusion. To get an acceptable fit, I increased the overextrusion allowance in the model to 0.5mm on all dimensionally critical surfaces to compensate for the "ludicrous speed" print settings.

In the course of printing the prototype, I noticed that the "lightening holes" that I incorporated into the print caused significant artifacts and slowed down the otherwise simple wall regions of the print. Running a model without the holes through my slicer, I was able to ascertain that not having the lightening holes used up a few extra centimeters of plastic, but shaved several minutes off of the printing time.

This is a good reminder of some important principles of quick and dirty design: Keep design details to a minimum, and make as many corners rounded as possible. These tips go hand in hand with a couple more: Make clearances as loose as practical, and allow adequate room for overextrusion.

With the useless and problematic lightening holes removed, I adjusted the design clearances to accommodate the base correctly and reprinted the part.

This time the pedal fit well, but another design flaw was noted – the overhang on the front was not long enough to accommodate a required stop mechanism to prevent the pedal from rising too much.

First test print. It didn't fit due to overextrusion, so I was really glad that I didn't waste 4 hours printing it! Note the crude but functional finish achieved with maximal nozzle overloading. The lightening holes on the vertical walls were removed, as they conferred almost no benefit and made printing slower. (Photo by author)

I designed a glue-on skirt to extend the part, and added a nice tread pad to give texture to the pedal surface. While I was at it, I added the optimal skirt length to the primary part, in case I ever wanted to print a whole new one.

Final design after all corrections. Simple shape, straight lines, and rounded corners help this design to print quickly and with few flaws despite high rate nozzle overloading. (Illustration by author)

As expected, the extreme settings caused interlayer adhesion to be a little weaker than normal, so I painted the assembly lightly with PVC-ABS pipe cleaner and let it dry for a couple of minutes. With the pedal strengthened, I painted it black and glued on the unpainted tread pad for a nice two tone effect.

The pedal worked well as designed, and the time spent prototyping and printing was reduced by more than 5 hours by using the "quick and dirty" printing techniques highlighted here.

The next time you have a non-critical part or a rough prototype to model, give it a try! It can save hours and a lot of needless frustration. The more moderate 25% over-width nozzle setting can also become a regular tool in your printing repertoire; enabling fast one-offs, high production rates for optimized models, less print failures, and reduced wear and tear on your printer as well.

Final result: A fully functional sewing machine control pedal. The crude finish from extreme nozzle overloading does nothing to diminish the utility of this very useful item. (Photo by author)

Recurve bow arrow rest:

A study in anisotropy

….or how to "make" $70 an hour with your 3D printer with this one weird trick.

In my never ending quest to be prepared for the inevitable zombie apocalypse, I was out practicing with my old recurve bow. The long tired Hoyt arrow rest finally gave way, and I went to Ebay to look into buying another one. I was about to click "buy it now" when I thought to myself…. Ok, so it's only a couple of dollars (for less than 1 gram of plastic)…but what if there were zombies outside, and I needed one today, not 2 weeks from now?

Thinking about the design, it was obvious that this could not be printed in one piece due to layer-wise anisotropy, the wood-like layerwise "grain" of the FFM printing process used on my RepRap printer. I designed the pieces to be printed flat on the bed, with no support or bed adhesion enhancement required.

The design is kept simple, with a low polygon count, to facilitate easy processing and printing while retaining all essential features.

For print speed and reliability, I optimized the design to be printed at 0.3mm layer height by checking my heights and keeping everything near a 0.3mm multiple in any critical structure. There are no overhangs more than 45 degrees, and no bridging is required in the design. This gives me 4 rests in about ten minutes on my old Prusa Mendel, using ABS.

I decided that for assembly, the rest would enter the base from the edge, using a slide – in dovetail joint. This should provide easy assembly and secure retention of the rest. Hopefully, the replacement rest "blades" would prove to be field installable so that one base could be reused many times, replacing only the "blade" that suffers the vast majority of abuses.

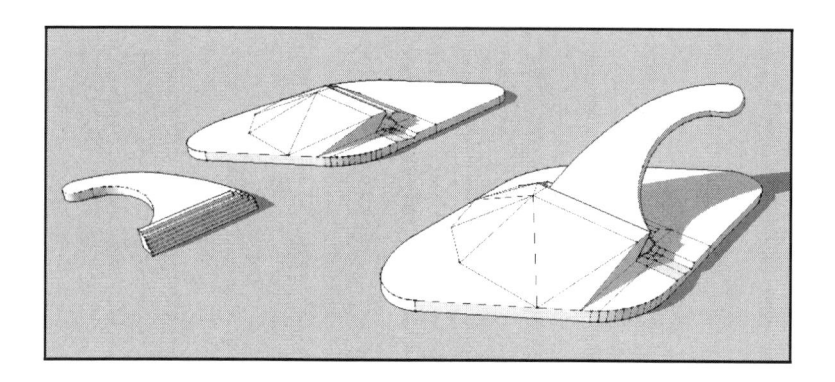

Final design of the recurve arrow rest. The base is to be printed in ABS, and the removable 'blade' in nylon. The design of the blade is constructed layer by layer, providing more precise control over the printing process at the expense of layer height flexibility. (Illustration by author)

I designed in 0.2mm of clearance in the joint to allow for dimensional error from over extrusion, while ensuring a snug fit.

I printed a few test units, modifying the design to fix any troublesome printing spots or design weakness. One of the critical changes was to close one end of the dovetail groove. On the first design this was open, which caused the groove to have inadequate reinforcement. This caused the blade to sometimes pull out of the slot during use.

After some test firing from my bow, I was unhappy with the durability of the ABS Blades. I set up some Taulman T-Glase (a PET plastic filament that prints well in most printers, only requiring 235 degrees at the nozzle) and printed some blades and bases from that.

The PET blades were much more durable, and though the PET bases are almost indestructible, the ABS bases were fine as is. The T-Glase prints best at about half the speed that I normally print ABS but since only the blades have to be printed in PET, the end result is still around 12 minutes for 4 blades - not counting the filament change time if you are using a single filament machine.

After taking the rests to the range with my local archery club, I had a chance to perform significantly more testing on the design. Overall results were good, but the rests still occasionally failed when arrows were shot with the incorrect nock orientation. By shooting the arrow effectively "upside-down", this causes the fins to strike the rest directly, with considerable force. This is not only a problem for 3D-printed arrow rests, it breaks injection molded ones as well. In order to further improve the product, I went back to the drawing board.

I optimized the blade support design for printing in nylon by modeling it in 0.3mm layers, so that the model design is precisely what will be printed. This enables more precise control of the printing process, as the slicer (Cura, in this case) has to make a lot less decisions about how to print the model. In effect, the model is "pre sliced" by the designer, because all the layers are expressly part of the design. This enables me to reduce the amount of retractions and "hopping" that the nozzle will do during printing, which is something that has caused me a lot of grief printing with nylon in the past.

While I was at it, I made some dimensional adjustments and added a locking tab to the base so the blades would be held more securely in place.

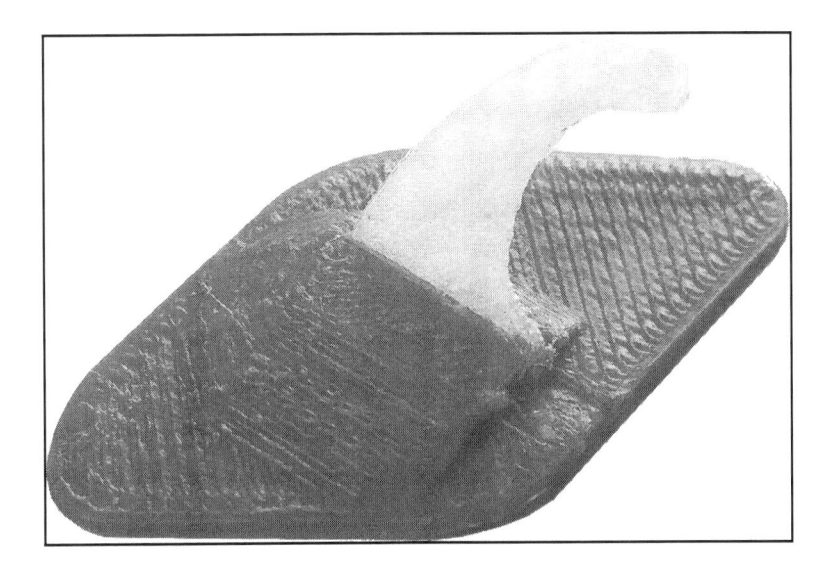

An assembled rest. These proved to be very durable, and functioned perfectly for their application in training bows. (Photo by author)

With an optimized design, I printed the blades in Taulman "Bridge" nylon, a filament with a low-for-nylon printing temperature of 242°C, and anhygroscopic and low shrinkage qualities (for nylon).

Like most nylons, Taulman Bridge is still troublesome to print with…..but better by a long shot than other nylons I have tried. (Authors note – the Taulman 910 nylon alloy prints even easier, but needs 245°C hot end temperature) Printing went well, and because of the flat nature of the design there were no unusual bed adhesion problems when using a little bit of white glue mixed with water on the bed.

The nylon blades are ridiculously resistant to damage, refusing to fracture or tear even with the "bite it and try to rip it in half with pliers" ISO9001 / ASTM approved testing method. No more blade failures were observed, at least within a few hundred shots.

In the end the best combination of print speed, economy, and utility was achieved with ABS bases and Taulman "Bridge" nylon blades. (Authors note – After using 910 alloy nylon, I expect that it would produce even better results) Material cost, even using the relatively expensive nylon, comes to around $0.05 USD per rest. If I print ten per build on my two machines I can build about 40 an hour, so at $2 each it's definitely worth doing. Now I just need to write a clickbait ad that says "this one weird trick makes $500 a day for people in (insert your location here) with a 3D printer – injection molding factories HATE it."

One piece Arrow Fins: Going against the grain

In this example, we have a demanding engineering challenge that defies the conventional methods of print optimization. After buying my millionth set of arrow fletching from Ebay, I started to think – how would I maintain my anti–undead archery skills without an endless supply of little plastic wings? I had printed some before but they proved to be fragile, and getting the glue off of the (expensive) carbon fiber arrow shafts was problematic. Worse, removing the damaged fletching and glue often damaged the shaft. What I needed was an easily replaceable fletching that I could print and install without glue.

This is a very challenging application. The part will be subjected to high loading, and must be strong and flexible, yet disintegrate gracefully upon severe impact without transferring damaging forces to the arrow shaft. It must be very lightweight yet impart sufficient aerodynamic forces to stabilize an arrow accelerating from 0 to 220mph (352kph) in less 2/3 of a meter. It must do all this, yet gracefully pass the hard obstructions of the arrow rest at over 100 meters per second, with about 4mm of clearance to spare.

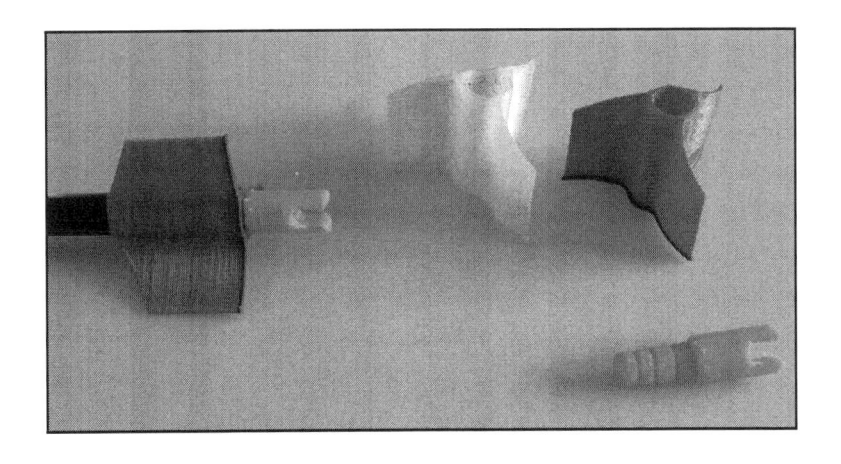

Arrow fletches and nocks in ABS and nylon (white). These proved to be very effective, easy to use, and cheap to print. Everything you could want when arming up for the next wave of post antigenic infected. (Photo by author)

I decided on a one piece design that slips over the back of the arrow, held in place by the nock. This way, if the fletches get damaged, I can just pop a new one on, no wear and tear on the arrow, no glue, no alignment issues... just pop and go. I already use a 3D printed arrow nock, a design that has proven to be adequate, if not quite as durable as its injection molded counterparts.

I should note that although this fletching design works for compound bows with full capture arrow rests, I doubt that this would work with conventional rests. Certainly it would be problematic with most recurve bows – especially anything without a center shot cutout. All of these archery related designs (and some really cool flying gliders) are available for download at threedsy.com.

In this design, I conspicuously ignore my regular advice of printing everything possible in the x-y plane of the print bed. There are several reasons for this. First and foremost is weight. A Suitable joint for adhering the fins to the carrier would add weight, as would glue. Weight is bad in modern archery, especially in the back of the arrow. A multi part fletching would add complexity, and a time consuming post print assembly process. This is meant to be a disposable part, and I want to invest the minimum possible proportion of non-robotic labor in its construction. Printing the vanes in the x-y plane would add a lot of strength – while this might seem good, in this case if the vanes hit something (at 350+kph) they are likely to be destroyed anyway. Excess strength here will only increase the chance of shattering the arrow, damaging the rest, or creating dangerous flying shards in the case of an incorrectly loaded arrow. Lastly, I want the vanes to be tolerant of partial failure. This design is nearly homogeneous on a layer by layer basis – so even if a portion is damaged, the damaged part can be picked off and the arrow shot again with only a slight reduction in performance.

The trickiest part of this design proved to be fine tuning the wall thicknesses and the printing parameters to get a fast printing, strong part.

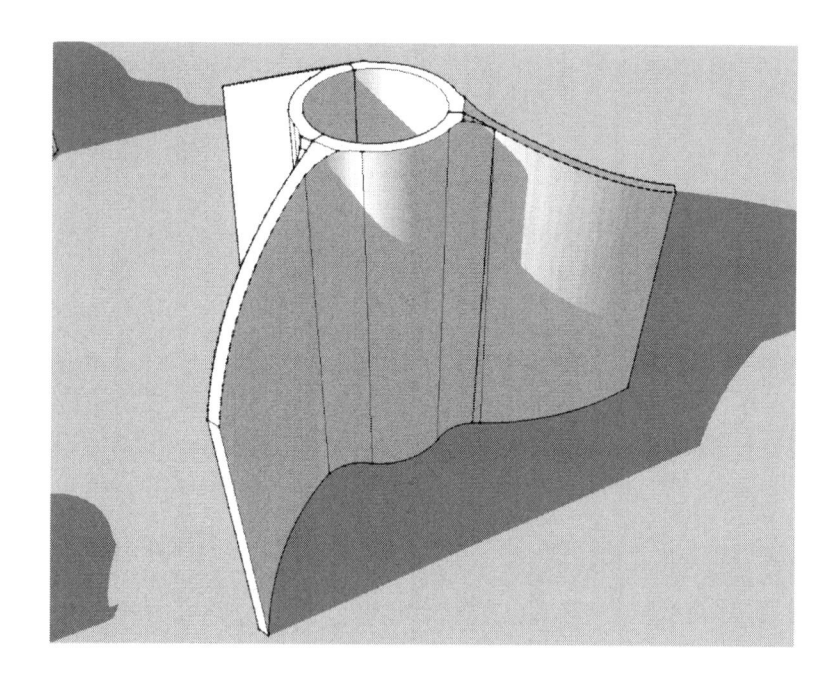

One of the final designs tested. When printed in nylon these proved to be extremely durable, convenient, and effective. (Illustration by author)

Sometimes when printing thin walled complex shapes, slicing software will make poor tool path decisions that can result in weak parts, poor finish, long print times, and even complete print failure. Just making things thicker (which usually works well) wasn't an option here, so playing with nozzle settings, shell thickness parameters, and model wall width was a significant part of the design task. Examining the tool path in CURA after each change allowed me to use trial and error to find an acceptable set of parameters. Hopefully, slicing software will get smarter and this will cease to be necessary.

A prototype was designed and printed in ABS, and did not fit properly, of course. I scaled the model to 105%, reprinted, and went on to field test it. For the first shot, I accidentally loaded the arrow upside-down. This destroyed the fletching and ejected the nock, but it did serve as an excellent test of the most important failure mode. The fletching separated from the arrow as designed and was mostly destroyed in a progressive disintegration, nicely absorbing most of the energy while not causing damage to the rest or creating missile hazards. So, with that out of the way, I loaded another and it shot nicely - grouping well with my other arrows. Satisfied with the basic concept, I went back to the drawing board to add some engineering finesse.

The result of shooting the arrow upside-down in a full capture arrow rest. The fletching performed as intended, detaching from the arrow without damaging the rest despite the high impact speed. (Photo by author)

The revised design, with a helical, twisted vane design spins the arrow, giving improved stability and improved crosswind performance. I printed some in ABS, as well as a few flexible and extremely tough ones from 910 alloy nylon. Even the ABS ones have proven to be remarkably durable, and the easy field replacement has been very successful. Overall, the model has met its design goals - it works well, shoots accurately, is cheap and fast to print, and is easy to replace in the field. Overall 10/10, will print more!

Appendix II:

Printing off the grid – Or,

3D Printing for preppers.

My office (and printing setup) is in a country where grid power is unreliable and not universally available. On the average, I have power (*that varies between 80 and 160 volts*) at my office for 6-12 hours every day.....except when I don't, for a few days. The 3D Printer at my workshop is powered 100% from solar power (as is the rest of my workshop). These experiences have given me some insights into optimizing 3D printing setups for alternative, unstable, or unreliable power.

__WARNING__: This section will make some suggestions that involve dealing with high current DC or high voltage AC power, or both. If you are not knowledgeable and practiced in this type of work, it is highly recommended that you ignore these *particular suggestions, or find someone who is qualified and / or licensed to help you carry them out. Really, you're probably just better off ignoring these options unless you were already thinking about them.*

It is also possible to do a good enough job on these tasks that they will work, but also to do them not quite good enough - so that they catch on fire days, weeks, or months later. If you don't understand exactly why, these recommendations are probably not for you.

In all cases, you must observe the requisite safety precautions inherent in electrical work, like making sure things are off and disconnected before working on them and the like. Remember, batteries are ALWAYS on.

In summary, you should not use your 3D printing setup as an introductory experiment in electricity, unless you enjoy being electrocuted, on fire, or both.

Not everyone can have a 'bot as zef as my old Prusa Mendel. This one has seen around a hundred kilograms of plastic pass through the hot end. (Photo by author)

Dealing with dirty power

In the best case, intermittent or irregular power can cause missed motor steps or controller reboots, ruining prints. In the worst case, power surges and spikes can destroy your power supply, or even your printer electronics.

A common solution is to use a regular (computer type) surge protector and uninterruptible power supply (UPS). This is a simple and effective solution for many systems, but it may not be ideal or even fully functional for all configurations. Some power supplies cannot fully drive the steppers through the (normally very quick) transition from line to back up power. This can cause skipped steps during the printing process, leading to misalignment of print layers. Normally this is a small offset, but sometimes even a small error is unacceptable, and in some cases the error may not be small.

To see if your backup system suffers from power failure anomalies, try unplugging your UPS from the wall several times during the printing of a test cube. If no artifacts or misalignment are produced, you are probably in good shape. It also may be instructive to see how long your UPS can power your printer before it shuts down. After your UPS has been plugged in for at least 24 hours continuously, you can unplug it during a print to test it and find out.

If you are in an area like mine with very unreliable or part-time power, a simple UPS is unlikely to be sufficient. In this case, you will probably have a battery and inverter system to power your home, office, or workshop when there is no power from the utility or a generator. This can be a very good solution, but many inverters have a switching time much slower than a standard UPS - which can (and usually will) cause print errors or failures. If you experience print errors when switching from line to battery power, or you are tired of losing a print when the inverter winks out waiting for you to start the generator, you have a few options.

WARNING: *some of these solutions (options 2 and 3) require connecting to the DC input side of your printer and will definitely void any warranty you may have. You should not try these options unless you are fully qualified to do so. If you aren't sure if you are qualified or not, then you probably aren't. If you happen to hook anything up backwards in these tasks, it will result in the smoke genie being released from your electronics. Electronics don't work again after the smoke genie leaves them. Also, the smoke genie frequently sets things on fire on his way out, being a vindictive jerk.*

Note: some of these modifications will require making connections on the high current DC side of your printer. I highly recommend making these connections using XT60 type or similar high amperage connectors, commonly used in RC cars and aircraft. They're inexpensive, reliable, and readily available in most areas or online. This will enable you to do all necessary wiring prior to hooking anything up, and you can recheck polarity before making any decisive connections. Also, it's really handy in general to have everything connectorized.

Option 1:

(Recommended, because you probably won't burn down your house this way)

>Use a commercial UPS system that works well both with your printer and gets along with your inverter, if you have one. It should be rated for at least 800 VA or more, depending on your printer specifications. This has the big advantage of being a non-technical solution that anyone can probably kludge their way through. Assuming that your printer will tolerate the nice short switching time of a UPS and that your inverter produces nice clean power, it's all plug and play. Also, it's almost guaranteed to not burn your shop down or electrocute you in the process of connecting it, even if you do it wrong.

Option 2:

(For electrical systems with a battery bank only)

If your printer runs completely off of DC power (usually 12 or 24V) using a power supply (most do!), and the operating voltage of your printer matches your main inverter battery bank, then you could run a line through a fuse or DC circuit breaker from the DC supply of your printer directly to the batteries. The advantages of this are:

- Most efficient (no losses from the inverter)
- Very solid power with no interruptions
- Less things to buy and to fail (no power supply needed!)

But it's not all roses. The principal disadvantage is that you will have to supply cabling for a 25 amp DC circuit, with line loss under one volt or so. In practice, unless the printer is within a couple of feet of the battery bank, this means using 6 or 8 gauge wire. Maybe even 4 gauge (or bigger) if the distance is over 35 feet. You should ideally consult a 5% wire loss table, but in general at 12 volts: 8 gauge up to 15 feet, 6 gauge to 25, and 4 gauge to 35 feet. You might be able to fudge this by 10 feet, depending on how much power your heated bed uses. For 24 volts, the distances can be twice as long, using the same wire gauge as stated for 12 volts.

Option 3:

If your power supply is a current regulated supply that can be adjusted to a nice multiple of 13.1 – 13.6 volts or so, you can wire a small (7AH or larger) lead acid battery in parallel between the supply and your printer. This is pretty convenient for 12V printers, but gets more complex for 24V types. You could also use a (20 amp or larger) fully automatic battery charger as a power supply, in line with the battery. There should be a fuse and switch between the supply and the battery as well as between the battery and the printer.

This configuration will allow you to use convenient AC power, while still being able to print for a couple of minutes during a transition to generator power or during regular switching events.

The disadvantages here are the same as option 1 as far as efficiency goes - a loss of 10-20% efficiency versus a system that connects directly to the main battery bank. The need to use a separate (small) battery just for the printer also ads to cost and complexity, and the addition of extra things to fail can be a factor.

Alternative power sources:

Wind, solar, hydro, and biogas generator based systems are nearly identical to the battery – inverter systems designed to handle intermittent power, so one of the intermittent power solutions above should meet your needs.

For mobile printing using a vehicle, I usually just have a 12V printer, and hook it directly to the 12V electrical bus of the vehicle. Cranking the starter can ruin prints, so be sure and pause your print before you crank the engine over. 24V vehicles would of course be easier to use with a 24V printer, but a DC-DC converter could be used for running a 24V printer in a 12V vehicle, or vice-versa.

The amperage requirements for bed heating are fairly high, so be sure your converter is big enough to handle the power requirements if you decide to use one. Of course, a small inverter could also be used to power an AC supply for your printer, and in many cases this might actually be the most cost effective solution.

I have seen solar panel based systems that worked directly from a panel, but I think this is a bad idea for many reasons. If you have a particular reason to think it is a good idea, I would remind you that lithium polymer batteries are cheap and light - as are the control circuits for them - and a 2200MAH or more 3 cell pack would do wonders for reliability. I use XT60 connectors on my printers anyway, so it would be trivial to hook up many off the shelf batteries.

The solar power installation at the author's remote office in the Caribbean. Note that the panels are above the normal reach of the infected. (Photo by author)

I think it might be interesting to use such a system with a lightweight battery and a panel along with a firmware modification that was aware of the system voltage. When voltage drops below a certain point, the print would pause, the filament would retract, and the print would stop, resuming when solar charging conditions allowed. That would make remote usage with minimal setups practical for larger prints. I will donate books (and any digital goods I offer) to anyone who does this and mentions this book in the source code comments, unless I write it first.

Glossary:

Additive Manufacturing

Additive Manufacturing describes any manufacturing process where material is deposited in a controlled way to incrementally manufacture the end product. Some examples of additive manufacturing are: 3D printing, some types of welding, and thin film deposition. This type of process is characterized by minimal waste, since raw material is deposited only where needed. The reciprocal process, subtractive manufacturing, is represented in conventional machining and woodworking, sheet cutting processes, and other methods where material is removed from an object to achieve the desired form. Subtractive manufacturing is typically characterized by a high waste ratio, as removed materials are frequently rendered unsuitable for further use.

Adhesion (bed)

Bed adhesion refers to the degree that a printed part adheres to the bed surface, allowing printing to continue. Bed adhesion can be enhanced by using bed covering materials or adhesives that are compatible with the material being printed.

Aliasing (errors)

In 3D printing, errors in the printing of a shape caused by the transition of one layer to the next. Very similar to pixelization or blockiness caused by resolution limitations in images. Aliasing errors in 3D printed objects are step-like artifacts from the layers in a print, and can be minimized by using a minimal layer height.

Anisotropic

Non-uniform, different in some dimensions than others. Anisotropy in 3D printing usually refers to the directional strength characteristics of printed parts that result from being constructed in layers. 3D printed objects tend to suffer from a lack of tensile strength in the Z-axis.

Artifacts, Artifacting

Small errors, usually extra lumps or bulges of extruded material caused by imperfections in the printing process. Artifacts can be minimized by proper printer calibration, thoughtful design, and good slicing software settings.

Bowden (extruder)

See Extruder (drive)

Bridging

Printing over a gap between two structures, without any supporting structures underneath.

Delamination

Part failure occurring from separation of layers at the layer boundary, caused by inadequate design, excessive strain, or poor layer fusion. Generally this occurs along the Z-axis of FFM parts. See Grain and Anisotropic.

Extruder (drive)

The component of the printer that drives the plastic into the heater and nozzle. The extruder can be directly mounted to the nozzle assembly, or remotely mounted utilizing a drive tube. The remotely mounted systems are known as "Bowden" type extrusion systems.

Extruder (nozzle)

The part of the printer that applies plastic to the working surface. Also known as an effector, nozzle, or tool. Sometimes referred to as the "hot end".

FFM, FDM® (additive manufacturing process)

Fused Filament Modeling or Fused Deposition Modeling®. The additive manufacturing process by which a filament is extruded and fused to build up an object being manufactured or repaired.

G-Code

Machine specific action instructions, usually involving motion or temperature control in the FFM context. G-code is used in many kinds of robotic manufacturing, and may include machine specific commands for any controllable machine function. G-code often includes a command and a parameter... for example, 'G28 x50 Y50' could mean to move the x and y machine axes to 50 machine units (often millimeters) from their zero positions.

Glass transition temperature, (floor)

The (lowest) temperature at which a material begins to act as a fluid. See thermoforming.

Grain

Anisotropic strength characteristic of 3D printed parts caused by the Z-axis layerwise tensile weakness. Superficially similar to the "grain" of wood.

Gussets, Ribs, Bosses

Design features used to give additional strength to structures. A gusset is an intersecting structure, usually triangular in form that offers cross-span support to another plane by anchoring it diagonally to another intersecting plane. A rib is similar to a gusset, except it typically spans the entire space between two parallel planes or walls, reinforcing them both. A boss is a raised area, typically used to support a fastener attachment point. In plastic manufacturing it is often braced to the rest of the structure by ribs or gussets.

Hygroscopic

A Hygroscopic material is one with an affinity for moisture. Hygroscopic plastics must be kept dry or dried out prior to use in 3D printers, or steam bubbles will be formed in the extruder while printing. This produces in a bubbly or even foamy extrusion, often resulting in poor print quality.

Infill

Algorithmically generated "filler" printing that prints inside the shell of a model, adding strength and support for successive layers.

Layer fusion

Adhesion by welding of one layer to the next in a 3D printed structure. Layer fusion is usually not quite as strong as the extrusion in other directions, giving rise to the anisotropic strength characteristics found in FFM printed objects.

Layer thickness (height)

The thickness that each extruded layer of a model is printed at. For example, a 1cm cube will consist of 50 printed layers if printed at a 0.2mm layer height. (See slicer, slice thickness)

Living Hinge

A simple hinge consisting of membrane spanning two parts to be hinged which flexes to accommodate the required motion.

Overextrusion

Surplus material deposited during the normal printing process. A slight surplus of extrusion that causes adjacent fibers to overlap and weld together during printing, resulting in a small increase in size of the part at its edges. For precision dimensions, the model should be undersized by one fourth to three fourths of the nozzle width setting in the X-Y plane.

Post Print Processing

Sanding, support material removal, assembly, or other processes required after printing to complete the manufacturing of a printed object.

Pre Print Processing, Pre-Processing (slicing)

Conversion of a 3D model into specific instructions (typically G-code) given to a manufacturing device such as a 3D printer to cause it to perform the actions necessary to manufacture the specified object.

Production stack (software)

A software system covering the end to end processing of data. In 3D printing, it could be an integrated system of design, slicing, and printing software. Not to be confused with the colloquial programming use of stack (as in "stack overflow"), which refers to a type of transient storage for data being processed.

Refactor, refactoring, factoring

Dividing a model into individual parts printed separately, to be assembled after printing is complete. This is usually done to allow printing each subcomponent in its ideal orientation for printability, strength, and printer size limitations. A primary paradigm for functional design, it is especially useful for optimizing strength and minimizing printing time.

Shell

The solid skin portion of a 3D printed object. In the X-Y plane, this is the number of solid perimeters in each layer. In the Z-axis, this is the number or thickness of solid layers at the upper and lower surfaces of a printed piece.

Slicer

A piece of software that processes a 3D model into a series of slices ascending along the Z-axis, and creates detailed instructions for operating the printing nozzle for each slice.

Slice thickness

The Z dimensional thickness of the slices that a 3D model is decomposed into by the slicing software (see slicer, layer thickness)

Support Material

Printed structures that are not intended to be part of the finished model, printed only to support other structures. Support structures will typically be manually removed or dissolved away in a solvent bath after printing.

Thermoforming

Molding, shaping, or forming a material at or above its glass transition temperature. When cooled, the material will retain its new form. Some printed plastics such as PLA can be easily thermoformed after printing by briefly immersing them in boiling water and forming them into the desired shape.

Warping (bed adhesion)

The tendency of some plastics, notably nylon and ABS, to warp and peel away from the bed during printing, causing distortion or print failure. Warping can be mitigated by design, print process changes (such as reducing layer cooling), and by the use of bed adhesion enhancers such as ABS-solvent slurry, hairsprays, or PVA glue.

About the author:

An early adopter of additive manufacturing and an innovator in the 3D printing space, I divide my time between my homes in Alaska and the Caribbean. My favorite authors include Neal Stephenson, Dewey Lambdin, George MacDonald Fraser, William Gibson, and Tom Robbins, to name a few. I am interested in pursuing collaborative projects in additive manufacturing, pervasive computing, and many other technology related fields.

Also, See my printable flying planes at threedsy.com, or check out some cool flying freebies at thingiverse.com/exosequitur

Haaarrrrr!

If you received this book courtesy of the incredible folks at the piratebay or other methods of sharing and found it worthwhile, consider supporting my creative endeavors by buying a paper or digital copy of this book, some of my designs at threedsy.com, buying me a good cup of coffee, or a decent lunch. I'm self published, and the sales of my books and designs are how I afford to be free to design and write.

If you cannot afford to contribute to my puny horde, please use this information to make the world a better place, mention the book to a friend with money, open source your designs, or build a sandcastle in my honor and send a photo to someone who has never seen the beach.

I, as well as my local constabulary, thank you in advance for keeping me off the streets.

BTC

Printed in Poland
by Amazon Fulfillment
Poland Sp. z o.o., Wrocław